Staying the Course

Fifteen Leaders Survey Their Past and Envision the Future of Churches of Christ

Edited by
Thomas H. Olbricht
Gayle M. Crowe

An Imprint of Sulis International
www.sulisinternational.com

Los Angeles | London

STAYING THE COURSE: FIFTEEN LEADERS SURVEY THEIR PAST AND ENVISION THE FUTURE OF CHURCHES OF CHRIST
Copyright ©2019 by Thomas H. Olbricht and Gayle M. Crowe. All rights reserved.

Except for brief quotations for reviews, no part of this book may be reproduced in any form or by any electronic or mechanical means, including information storage and retrieval systems, without written permission from the publisher. Email: info@sulisinternational.com.

Library of Congress Control Number: 2019909258
ISBN (print): 978-1-946849-58-8
ISBN (eBook): 978-1-946849-59-5

Published by Keledei Publications
An Imprint of Sulis International
Los Angeles | London

www.sulisinternational.com

Words like "identity crises" have become a frequent refrain in contemporary churches of Christ. Crises or not, this book is an opportunity to sit down with 15 of the wisest, most interesting old heads our heritage has to offer—who while not uncritical, decided to stay. This book is an act of love and devotion to God and church. If I wanted to spend an evening discussing the travails and triumphs of churches of Christ, I cannot imagine a more engaging group of men and women. This book is as close as you can get to having them sitting around your living room!

> — Randy Harris
> Spiritual Director, College of Biblical Studies, Abilene Christian University

As children, we learned the power of a story. While being cuddled on a lap a loved one, we were taken to imaginary places, on great adventures, and into the depths of the emotional highs and lows of our family lore. While engulfed in a story, one was safe to ask questions like "what if?" and "could it be?".

In this book are fifteen stories of men and women who have chosen to live their lives in the story of God. Most would agree that there is a fresh wind blowing in His story. More people are using their experience of life as a pathway to God rather than using God to improve their experience of life. These are the stories of a community of God's people who have experienced life to its fullest while engaging the antecedents in scripture as their compass. As leaders of this group, the Spirit has blown over them in mighty ways, and these men and women here share their experiences of highs and lows of God working in His world.

So cuddle up, enjoy remembering or hearing for the first time the lore of a part of God's family but don't ever forget to keep asking the question, "What is God doing here?"

> — Rhonda Lowry, M.Div., Lipscomb University

As I read this delightful collection of memoirs, I was reminded of the importance of a path in scripture's wisdom literature. We are urged to stay on the path — the place worn by the traffic of godly people who have come before. In these stories of older believers, there is a memory of who "we" (in Churches of Christ) have been at our very best -- along with an admission of some of our failures. And along with that memory, there is a hopeful trajectory as we imagine what may lie ahead. What a privilege to listen in to these accounts of the work of God in such diverse lives!

> — Mike Cope, Director of Ministry Outreach, Pepperdine University

Contents

Preface i

Foreword iii

Success to Significance: When Old School Was Cool by Janice Brown 1

A Memoir and Vision for the Church by Alfred Darryl Jumper 11

My Life in the Churches of Christ by Richard Hughes 17

Crossroads: A Personal Journey by Jack Scott 27

Memoirs and Vision by Fred D. Gray 37

Back in the Day by Paul Watson 53

A Recall of Personalities, Opportunities, and Involvements by Andrew J. Hairston 63

Let Me Tell You a Story by Robert Randolph 73

Looking Back by Lynn Anderson 85

Roads More Traveled by Tom Olbricht 97

Sing On by Carolyn Hunter 107

The Least of His Servants by Dwain Evans 117

Correcting Mistakes and Keeping the Faith in a Dominant Left-Wing PC Culture That Is Virulently Anti-Christian and Anti-Rational by J.J.M. Roberts 127

Memoirs by John T. Willis 139

Memoirs of an Old Ball Player by Gail E. Hopkins 149

Contributors

Lynn Anderson Minister. Founded Hope Network Ministries. Author of thirteen books.

Janice Brown Attorney. Retired Court of Appeals Judge, Washington D.C.

Dwain Evans. Minister. Initiator of "exodus movements" in Churches of Christ. Homebuilder.

Fred D. Gray Attorney. Lawyer for Rosa Parks, Martin Luther King, Selma March.

Andrew Hairston. Minister. Retired Chief Judge of City Court of Atlanta, GA.

Gail E. Hopkins. Professional baseball player. Orthopaedic surgeon. University Boards.

Richard Hughes Professor Emeritus at both Pepperdine University and Messiah College.

Carolyn Hunter Professor, Humanities Division, Pepperdine University.

Alfred D. Jumper. Director, Pediatric Anesthesiology, Specialty Surgical Center, Beverly Hills.

Thomas H. Olbricht Distinguished Professor Emeritus of Religion, Pepperdine. 25 books.

Robert Randolph. MIT Senior Associate Dean for Student Life, Chaplain. Minister.

J.J.M. Roberts Professor of Old Testament Emeritus, Princeton Theological Seminary.

Jack Scott Chancellor, California Community Colleges. Served on California Assembly.

Paul Watson Minister. Professor of Biblical Studies, Austin Graduate School of Theology.

John T. Willis. Retired Professor, Abilene Christian University. Elder, Highland Church.

We dedicate this book to David Fleer who has creatively and inexhaustibly parlayed the annual Thomas H. Olbricht Christian Scholars Conference into a major venue for Christian academic dialogue. David offered major input into the making of this volume. We salute you, David, for your vision and productive service to the Kingdom.

Preface

In the summer of 2015, David Fleer (Professor of Homiletics at Lipscomb University and Director of the Thomas H. Olbricht Christian Scholars' Conference) asked me to breakfast. His challenge: "In the fellowship of Churches of Christ are many incredible men and women of faith. However, one by one the obituaries are coming, and these leaders of faith are slipping away. And the sad part is, for the most part, nobody knows their stories. Oh, we know what they have become, but we don't know the stories of what made them what they became. Is there a way to tell their stories?"

Before we left breakfast, we had determined the overall parameters for selecting some of these church leaders to highlight during the next three years of the annual Thomas H. Olbricht Christian Scholars' Conference. Their expertise might be in a variety of fields—but each one would be recognized as a leader in Churches of Christ. They must be aged seventy or above. Each would have earned the terminal degree in his or her field. Each would be asked to write a 3,000-word autobiography. And then each would be offered the opportunity to peer into the distance ten—twenty—thirty years to write another five hundred words about what they envision that the future of Churches of Christ might be.

Over the next three years, fifteen men and women of faith read their "Memoirs and Vision" at the Thomas H. Olbricht Christian Scholars' Conference held in Nashville, Tennessee. In this volume, all fifteen essays are presented. Each is alike in that we see the power and the working of God in the life of each. But no two are alike because God acted in the lives of each one uniquely according as He determined. Wrote Paul to the Corinthians,

"I came to you in weakness and fear, and with much trembling. My message and my preaching were not with wise and persuasive words, but with a demonstration of the Spirit's power, so that your faith might not rest on men's wisdom, but on God's power."

Which is to say, there are no self-made Christians! Every woman or man who submits to the Lordship of Jesus Christ is thereby placed under the power of God. And that means nobody—but nobody—can predict the outcome of that Christian's life! "God moves in a mysterious way," as every Christian biography can attest.

You, the reader, are in for a treat. These authors are attorneys, ministers, judges, medical doctors, businessmen, and college professors. The personality of each writer is evident. In every case, they had to overcome obstacles in order to stay the course in Churches of Christ, while remaining faithful to their Lord.

By the time you reach the last page, you will have witnessed the work of God in fifteen distinct ways in order to create for His Kingdom fifteen servants whose lives have blessed many. And perhaps, just perhaps, you will start to see your own life in a different way as you allow your Creator to continue His work in you!

Gayle Crowe

Foreword

The individuals who have written their personal histories and their vision for Churches of Christ in this book are different. Why are they so unusual? They are professional people: judges, medical doctors, lawyers, ministers, businessmen, and professors. According to sociologists as well as according to conventional wisdom, professionals are social climbers. As they ascend the ladders of success, they transfer from one type of church to another. They start out as conservatives, then move into evangelical circles; in a few years they join mainstream Presbyterians and finally become Episcopalians. The fifteen professionals of these autobiographies defy the conventional. They stayed the course.

Why are their stories so important? These narratives are significant because these women and men have been the perennial backbones of numerous congregations among the Churches of Christ. They have been elders, ministers, class teachers, and opinion leaders. Anyone drawn to history will want to read these narrations. From these autobiographies, readers will apprehend the real inside history of Churches of Christ. They will ponder over the aspirations and actions of steadfast leaders. They will empathize over tribulations and victories. They will obtain a more in-depth sense of where the Churches of Christ have been and where they are heading. Readers whose ages are concomitant with those of the authors will, upon reading these statements, reminisce regarding their own religious upbringing.

The writers of these narratives have been involved in many regions of North America and the world. Their experiences range from Massachusetts to Malibu, from Canada to the Carolinas, from Arizona to Alabama, from California to Connecticut, from Augusta to Austin, and from Dallas to Denver. The narrators have been involved with churches from Buenos Aires to Brussels, from São Paulo to St. Petersburg, and from Christ Church to Cambridge. Though many of the authors grew up in areas of Churches of Christ predominance, they demonstrated their convictions and skills to the distant islands.

While families of some of the writers weren't Churches of Christ at first, in every case, at some stage in their youth, parents or relatives who were members encouraged, or reinforced the decision of these authors to place their lives into the fellowship of a devoted congregation. In many instances, the writers' mothers were the major encouragers. In some cases, women Bible class teachers wielded a significant inspiration. In other cases, dedicated servant leaders in the congregation became important exemplars. In some situations, the preacher for the congregation exhibited unusual Christ-like characteristics. None of these authors mentioned the impact of a youth minister. They grew up in the years before youth ministers became common. All the narrators alike expressed appreciation for the impact of the congregations in which they were nurtured.

I have, through the years, been especially impressed with those who decided to stay the course. Every last one of them could have left. They made an irrevocable choice to stay. I myself have been invited to leave, both by those not of Churches of Christ, and those who are.

In 1955 I took a position at the University of Dubuque in Iowa that had strong ties with the Presbyterian Church. University Presbyterian Church was adjacent to the campus, and many of the administrators and faculty were members. We lived in a University house only two blocks from the church building. I was asked by an administrator or two if I would consider becoming a member of University Presbyterian. They pointed out that membership would enhance my status at the University in various ways. I thanked them but stated that I had strong ties with Churches of Christ and much preferred to continue with my own heritage. That I did so didn't cause major problems. I served on the Chapel Committee even if the chair, an older Presbyterian Bible Professor, was a bit wary of me and never asked me to lead a prayer at the start of the committee meetings.

Foreword

In 1962 we moved to State College, Pennsylvania, where I held a Speech Professorship. We lived in a new development north of the city called Park Forest Village. The one church in the development was a United Brethren congregation. Several families who lived in the Village were members at that church including one of my Penn State colleagues. He and his family lived not far from us and we became good friends. He was something of a leader at the congregation and invited me to deliver the sermon one Sunday, which I did. He later asked if I would consider becoming a member of the congregation since they needed some strong leadership. I declined again by affirming the commitment of Dorothy and me to Churches of Christ.

I now turn to two concrete times in which I was invited to leave Churches of Christ by members, though I have received similar invitations in letters. Early in my Abilene Christian years, I spoke at a lectureship session on Bible texts. I presented 1 Corinthians 15 on the resurrection. I stated that according to Paul, the Christian hope for eternal life is resurrection from the dead in a new body. I said that whereas Plato wrote at length about the immortality of the soul, that specific terminology is not found in Scripture. I was on a high platform in Moody Coliseum and almost immediately after the session was over, I was surrounded by a half dozen persons. It was mainly an older woman who spoke. She declared that I wasn't teaching Church of Christ doctrine and if she believed what I did she would leave the church, and furthermore, she declared that I should do so. I told her that in my church background, I had been taught that we needed to follow the truth from the Scriptures even if it was contrary to what the preachers conventionally stated. I told her that what I said was from Paul in 1 Corinthians and as a good Church of Christ member that was what I planned to teach. Later I heard some reports of displeasure with what I said, but no one at ACU called me on the carpet for my presentation.

In the 1980s, I began to teach and write on interpreting the Scriptures, that is, hermeneutics. I proposed that from the standpoint of Scripture itself, the best interpretation brings us face to face with the living God, The Father, the Son, and the Holy Spirit. I declared that focusing on God gave us a more true meaning of the Word than did commands, examples, and necessary inferences. According to some conventional thought leaders in the church, I was no longer teaching Church of Christ doctrine and should leave.

I was invited to speak on hermeneutics at several locations in Ontario, one of which was Beamsville. Before the first session, I was approached privately by a man about thirty. He said he was in the army, but he was going to muster out, attend a preachers' school, and start preaching. He showed me a legal pad and a ballpoint pen. He told me he was going to report every word I said and write me up. I told him that he was welcome to do exactly that. I planned to speak on what I understood the Bible to teach on hermeneutics and intended to do so regardless of his threat because I had been told that in Churches of Christ we teach whatever we find in the Bible even if it differs with what some have previously taught. Our charge is to be true to the word. I told him furthermore that I was a member of the Churches of Christ before he was born, and I intended to continue being a member long after he was gone. I suspect he was charged to report on my "heresy" by an editor of one of our periodicals. I noticed him writing vigorously during the first session. The second session, he only jotted down items sporadically. By the third session, I didn't see the yellow pad. He just sat listening. I never saw any write up about the sessions or my heresies. This man didn't know what to make of what I said, or else he decided I wasn't so off the wall Biblically after all. I decided long ago to put my hand to the plow and not turn back. I am therefore a great admirer of those who have stayed the course. I salute those who narrated their dedicated journey for this volume.

I have intentionally refrained from summarizing the various visions offered by these writers for the future of the church. Readers need to apprehend the visions based upon the context out of which the various writers came to them. I encourage you to carefully weigh the authors' hopes and dreams for the future. Their track record of sticking it out for a lifetime means that these writers warrant a hearing.

> *Finally brothers and sisters, whatever is true, whatever is honorable, whatever is just, whatever is pure, whatever is lovely, whatever is commendable—if there is any moral excel-*

lence and if there is anything praiseworthy—dwell on these things. (Philippians 4:8 (CSBBible)

Thomas H. Olbricht

Success to Significance: When Old School Was Cool
by Janice Brown

Awe. When I was young, the word "awe" was not part of a colloquialism expressing delight or satisfaction. These days everything is "awesome." In those days, awe was the description of a humble state of reverence; a response to the fearsome might of the Creator that froze our speech and compelled obeisance. It was reason enough to abase ourselves—facedown and mute, groveling in the dust—before an infinite majesty that outstripped our most vivid and terrible imaginings. In C.S. Lewis' classic, *The Screwtape Letters,* the demon mocks the tendency of Christians to pray as if God "was actually *located*—up and to the left at the corner of the bedroom ceiling"—as if this prosaic spot had anything to do with the reality of God. But, that was not the God I encountered in Luverne, Alabama, in the middle of the last century.

Tucked among the towering pines, my grandparents' tiny house looked across a long sweep of the Alabama foothills. I could watch the summer lightning arc across the horizon; see the rain sweeping toward me, a misty curtain that raised the sweet, pungent aroma of dampened dust just before it obscured the landscape and drummed on the roof. The Rural Electrification Project of TVA had not yet come to our little cul-de-sac. The night that fell on our isolated section of the Mt. Ida Highway was absolute. On those pitch-black nights, without the benefit of street lights, the darkness revealed a dense thicket of stars, wheeling above my head in such wonderful profusion that I lost all sense of being earthbound. From the wide seat of a white-washed swing, anchored between two sturdy pines, I could tilt my head back and cross the universe with 50-meter strides; swim laps in the Milky Way. Or focus more intimately on the squadrons of fireflies that flitted around the yard. The surroundings blackness harbored a breath of the numinous, a soft exhalation of otherness, of clawed feet or angel wings —who could say? Perhaps it was proximity to a more primitive understanding of the world that allowed an openness to a reality beyond the mundane.

At age six, I was given a copy of *The Golden Treasury of Bible Stories*. The volume was published in 1954. I have it still and for a book now more than 60 years old, it is in good condition—though well-worn as any Bible should be. This book, the editor says, tells some of the most important stories of the Bible from the beginning of the world to revelation. Though the book is written for children, there is nothing condescending or diffident about the stories interpreted. I liked the parables and pondered the miracles; however, it was the Old Testament that captured my imagination. The power and poetry of Genesis and Job, Jacob's ladder of angels, Moses in the bulrushes, the burning bush, the parting of the Red Sea, the Ten Commandments written by the finger of God, Elijah calling devouring flames from the sky and then being carried away in a chariot of fire. Other youngsters might have learned about righteous wrath, justice, and the consequences of evil from Marvel Comics or Radio Classics. But my super-hero was the God of the Old Testament and those He befriended. This God who spoke the world into existence; this being the Christian liturgy describes as "God of God, Light of Light" and truth was a God "mindful of man" and willing to rescue his people from bondage. For a solitary colored girl who was often lost in the contemplation of the cosmos, this was a pivotal insight though it took me a lifetime to understand it. The flight from Egypt was an object lesson that never ceased to resonate, like the choruses of sorrow songs we never sang in our fellowship. "Tell ole, Pharaoh, let my people go." Or songs the Baptist sang: "Oh Mary don't you weep; tell Martha not to moan. Pharaoh's army got drownded."

Looking back, I can see that it was my fascination with the compelling narratives of *The Golden Treasury* that began my love affair with books, with the written word, with truth and the ideal of freedom, and ultimately shaped my vocation.

My family had attended the Church of Christ for generations. I would not describe myself as a cradle-Campbellite. I did not study the Restoration Movement until I was a young adult. The church was simply the background and culture of my early life. My parents had met in church; my grandparents on both sides were members of the church; and my maternal grandmother, whose maiden name was Kolb, confirmed that her parents had been members of the Church of Christ. Since my grandmother was born in the late 1800s, it is conceivable that the Kolb's affiliation with the Churches of Christ reached back to at least the era of Reconstruction. My grandparents' generation had little formal education, but my grandmother's brother, James Kolb, was a well-respected Bible teacher—a formidable debater—and a civil rights activist long before activism was cool.

It was from James Kolb (my Uncle Bubba) that I learned respect for rigorous argument. I came to understand that we were "people of the book" and that it behooved us to know that book and to examine all doctrine to assess its consistency with the Bible. Many evenings were spent developing the theme that we were privileged to be part of the one true church. In those days the Church of Christ was unapologetic about its exclusivity. But that is not to say such discussions were mean-spirited. Rather, I had the sense that men like my uncle (and other old warriors like Marshall Keeble) considered it a privilege to argue converts into heaven. The loving genuineness of Marshall Keeble's altar calls sometimes elicited hundreds of responses. What later generations would condemn as rigid legalism, ministers and teachers in those confident days saw as their duty to save the benighted.

No moral relativism practiced in the homes where I spent my childhood. There was right and wrong, good and evil. Fear God and seek understanding was the watchword. We went to church twice on Sundays and again on Wednesday. A certain mental and physical toughness was expected. If you stubbed your toe and took a significant and bloody chuck out of your toenail as often happens when you go barefoot, you were told after the damage had been duly inspected to "get over it!" Most people were poor. Folks did not have much stuff. It was a time and place where what you could purchase mattered much less than character and reputation. The rules for life were uncomplicated: "Do work hard; keep your word; strive for excellence in everything you do. Do unto others…even when they don't do unto you. Don't lie, cheat, steal, beg; don't envy. And whatever you do, don't snivel."

There was an ominous and insistent theme that ran beneath my seemingly carefree childhood. A single, sustained, menacing note that slid in and out of consciousness as swiftly and silently as a switchblade. In the 1950s, you could feel an alertness in the air like the first smell of smoke from a distant fire. Despite the fact that my family's roots were already generations deep in that southern soil, we were not quite welcome and not quite citizens. Though we were familiar, a fixture, and a political touchstone, we were also alien and despised. To some people we were a burden; to others a threat. It was a peculiar existence and there were austere rules—even in the fellowship. I attended a Black church and a segregated school. Education, both spiritual and secular, was a necessity. But I never drank from the colored fountain, used the colored restroom, or sat in the colored waiting room at the bus station, and I certainly never went to see a movie where I would be relegated to the colored balcony which meant I never went to the movies at all. Life was structured to avoid these indignities. If we traveled, we packed a hearty lunch. If we went to town, we were sternly warned there would be no bathroom breaks until we returned home. Extreme youth would not earn you any dispensation.

Brown v. *The Board of Education* was decided in May 1954. Emmett Till was murdered in Mississippi in August 1955. Some people said that it was a murder that started a movement. The bus boycott that began in Montgomery in December 1955 was part of the daily conversation of those who sat on our front porch in the cool of the evening, speaking their determination into being. When Rosa Parks refused to give up her seat, she said Emmett Till—whose death had been the subject of a recent lecture at her church—was on her mind. By December 1956, boycotters had brought the Montgomery transit system to the brink of insolvency, and a federal court declared, in *Browder v. Gayle*, that the segregation of public transit was unconstitutional. That same year Arthurine Lucy was allowed to enroll as a graduate student in Library Science at the University of Alabama. It had taken a court case, *Lucy v. Adams*, to pave the way. She was the first black person ever admitted to a white public school or university in the state of Alabama. She lasted three days. On the third day of classes, a hostile mob prevented Lucy from attending classes and the University suspended her on the ground that they could not provide a safe environment—the same excuse universities give these days for banning conservative speakers from campus!

Without any doubt, my heart was forged in the fires of those years. All around me I saw tenacity and persistence in the face of seemingly insuperable odds. A rock-bound faith brought courage to the sticking point. Alabama was thick with civic clubs and improvement associations. Ordinary people took extraordinary risks. I developed a lasting affinity for the warrior virtues: courage, valor, self-sacrifice. I do not rehearse this history to scrape the scabs off old wounds or incite rage against America. I am emphatically not part of the "blame America first" crowd. I love this country. I am convinced it is—as Lincoln said—"The last best hope of Earth." God has promised to "make all things new" (Rev. 21:4,5). Until then, American constitutionalism—on proper principles—offers the only blueprint for human flourishing. America is not perfect. There can be no perfect country unless it is a country with no people in it. The choice is not between good and better. The choice is between a religiously hostile and, silly, suicidal culture and what Eliot dubs a "religious and necessarily imperfect" one.

You cannot have a heritage that includes, as mine does, not only the middle passage but the trail of tears; not only the rhythms of midnight trains but the terrors of midnight riders, Jim Crow and Jim Dandy, without contemplating how law and morality intersect. And anyone with that kind of history will tell you quite emphatically that the positive law is not enough. Never enough. When I was growing up, the positive law declared some people more equal than others. But that law, judged by a higher law, was wrong. Moral values must be at the core of a liberal democratic regime. As C.S. Lewis puts it: "A dogmatic belief in objective value is necessary to the very idea of a rule which is not tyranny or an obedience which is not slavery."[1] We must, as Arthur Leff once noted, either be ruled by the great I AM, or we must submit ourselves to the great SEZ WHO.

Before I reached my teens, I was deeply committed to the impartial rule of law and acutely aware of the suffering caused by the failure to adhere to those ideals. These experiences turned my thoughts toward the law. In the abstract, my family appreciated the legal victories of those early days and applauded the courage of the lawyers who worked to achieve them. But in the everyday world, dealing with lawyers usually meant big trouble. In fact, I think I was eight or nine years old before I realized that "shyster lawyer" was two words. It was not that my family thought I could not be successful. They were convinced (and they convinced me) that I could do or be anything I chose. They questioned whether it was possible to be both a successful lawyer and a good human being. What finally reconciled them to this general idea was the life and career of Fred Gray. Fred Gray was the lawyer who filed the suit in *Browder v. Gayle* and won it. He represented Rosa Parks and he was Martin Luther King's Alabama counsel. But much more important from my family's point of view, Fred Gray was also a preacher and a member of their faith tradition. That at least proved anecdotally the existence of one good lawyer who was also a good man. Of course, the question of whether I too could be a minister of the gospel did not arise. That path was not open to me.

I was a freshman in college when the Revolution of 1968 set off the long march of leftist radicals through American institutions. The Weather Underground promised to "destroy everything good and decent in America," and by 1978 they had succeeded in capturing the academy and beginning the process—now reaching its apogee—of dismembering the American creed, restoring tribalism, exalting identity politics, reverse engineering racism, and scourging religion from the public square.

At America's core was an idea about freedom. Even our institutions of government were inspired by Christianity. The division between spiritual and temporal authority, the insight that elicited the fundamen-

---

[1] C.S. Lewis, *The Abolition of Man* (1944), 73.

tal features of the liberal democratic order—limited government and individual rights—came about "not in rebellion against religion, but in defense of religion against the encroachment of the state."[2] The grounding of religious freedom was *not* an expression of personal autonomy; it was rather an inference from the sovereignty of God. In the words of James Madison: "It is the duty of every man to render [homage] to the Creator…and [this] duty is precedent, both in order of time and degree of obligation to the claims of Civil Society."[3]

While the Christian worldview dominated our political consciousness, we demanded limited government and revered negative freedom—the right to speak our minds, worship as we chose, have our property protected, and pass on our ideas of the good life to our children. Christian charity was a personal responsibility. Once the secular worldview achieved preeminence, government was transformed into a permissive cornucopia—issuing an endless stream of positive rights. The culture war that began with the Sexual Revolution of the 1960s has come to an end. Christianity lost decisively. As Ephraim Radner, an Anglican theologian observes: "There is no safe place in the world or in our churches within which to be a Christian. This is a new epoch."[4]

For at least a decade the Churches of Christ have been mired in an identity crisis. Much of our corporate energy has been focused on defining the brand. Has our uniqueness been reduced to singing acapella in four-part harmony? The sense of stability and certainty of the mid-century church is long gone. Some think we have abandoned our core identity; others complain that our rigid traditionalism prevents us from being relevant to a culture desperately in need of the gospel.

---

[2] Michael W. McConnell, *Why Religious Liberty is the First Freedom,* 21 CARDOZO L. REV. 1243, 1244 (2000)

[3] James Madison, "Memorial and Remonstrance against Religious Assessments," reprinted in *5 THE FOUNDER'S CONSTITUTION 82 (Phillip B. Kurland & Ralph Lerner eds., 1987) (1785).*

[4] Ephraim Radner, "No Safe Place Except Hope: The Anthropocene Epoch," *Living Church,* July 28, 2016, http://livingchurch.org/covenant/2016/07/28/no-safe-place-except-hope-the-anthropocene-epoch/.

But we have bigger problems. We are living in a world that is not only post-Enlightenment but post-Christian. The culture is relentlessly hostile. So are many of those in the pews. They are our children. In the ancient world, Budziszewski tells us, "the people who needed to be evangelized were outside the walls of the church; today they include thousands who are inside but who think just like those outside. When the gospel is proclaimed, they complain."[5]

While all of these issues are real and challenging enough to consume our energies for the next decade, they pale in comparison to the high probability that real persecution is in store for committed Christians. Realistically, a religious test already exists for public office. The protection for religious freedom has been excised from the constitution and the coalition that passed the Religious Freedom Restoration Act (RFRA) could never be reconstituted in the current political climate. Antidiscrimination laws now trump the Constitution. Business owners are already being driven out of the marketplace by lawsuits and ruinous fines. Regulations tied to government funding will continue to put pressure on church-affiliated schools to comply with regulations that flatly contradict Christian anthropology—not to mention common sense. They are already ashamed of the gospel; soon they will deny it outright.

The Trump presidency has given the church time to exhale. The reprieve is likely to be brief. No doubt it will be hard to be the marginalized minority, but it may save us. We must cease to make an idol of Caesar. We can start schools; strengthen our faith communities; strive for deeper friendships with other believers; rediscover and exercise the ordinary, "everyday elements of moral character"[6] like fortitude, temperance, forbearance. We might rediscover the mystery of *The Holy*,

---

[5] J. Budziszewski, The Underground Thomist, *Optimism, Pessimism, Neither of the Above?* http://www.undergroundthomist.org/optimism-pessimism-neither-of-the-above?

[6] J. Budziszewski, The Underground Thomist, *Optimism, Pessimism, Neither of the Above?,* http://www.undergroundthomist.org/optimism-pessimism-neither-of-the-above?

the God who engenders fear and trembling and enchantment; the God who in Ulrich Lehner's phrase is "not nice."

I'd like to end on a personal note. I saw it from a hill in Malibu overlooking the Pacific. And I finally understood. From that spot, in the early morning, there is a path across the sea; a fiery, reflective road like burnished copper. No wonder the ancients spoke of chariots of the sun. That fiery path across the sea led straight to a spot on the horizon, a fierce and breathtaking incandescence too bright for my eyes. Too good for my eyes. I had to look at it sidelong. And the beauty of it was like a wave, a pulse of radiance washing over me, dazzling my senses, exhilarating my heart, until I drown in it. And I think this is how God must be. A light too bright, benign and terrible, too good for my eyes. A light my limited imagination cannot bear. A pure, perfect, incandescent glory for which I long, to which I belong. And here's the best part. Nothing—not the unutterable blackness of my soul or yours, nor all the greed, malice, arrogance, or pettiness of our stunted hearts can dim that light one iota. That is the miracle of the incarnation, the resurrection, and the omnipotent, immutable "I AM." Not all the darkness of our evil hearts—of a million billion evil hearts—can cause that light to flicker or fluctuate. And I think I understand Lucifer—his name means light—and how he felt not just jealousy but despair. For the Creator—the one who lights all the suns; the one who laid earth's cornerstone "[w]hen the morning stars sang together";[7] the force that unfurled the universe—that source of all light—battles the darkness for love, not power. And so should we.

---

[7] Job 38:6-7 (King James Version).

A Memoir and Vision for the Church by Alfred Darryl Jumper

My mother grew up in the Church of Christ, as did her mother. It is little wonder that I, too, followed in their footsteps and trod a path to the same church. For most of us who grew up in our community in North Tulsa, Oklahoma, in the 1950s, going to church was not an option. It was a requirement. I remember bitterly cold winters when my mom would wake up early Sunday morning, put on a pot of coffee, put a Mahalia Jackson record on the record player, and set up the ironing board. As she ironed our clothes, she would wake us one by one so that we could bathe and eat breakfast before she left for church with my eight siblings and me in tow. In retrospect, I suppose that was the genesis of my not-so-recently changed perspective, which has afforded me a love-infused patience for those who show up late for the worship service. I think about what my mother went through to get us to church and I see now that I, like most of my brothers and sisters who just happened to have arrived on time, don't have a clue as to what others had to go through in order to arrive when they did. And while I am not condoning being late (personally, I abhor it), it is truly amazing how much more relaxed and enjoyable a worship experience can be when your attitude toward others says, "I'm just glad to see you, (no matter what time you arrived)."

My early years in the church, from the early 1950s until I left Tulsa in 1970, were significant for many reasons, not the least of which is that it was there that I met a man whom I describe to this day as, without question, the finest man I have ever known. His name was Leon Meachem, and he and his family were very close to my mom and her family as they were growing up. That relationship stayed strong until the day he died, May 25, 1988. Like most of us who grew up in that place and time, Brother Meachem, by most standards, didn't have the proverbial "pot to piss in or window to throw it out of" and yet he taught me, by example, the meaning of giving. Somehow, not knowing that you are poor makes it eminently more tolerable. Despite a poverty that sometimes bordered on penury, he amassed a wealth that only givers can possibly know. And he taught me to do the same. When the school counselor (who was white) at my then-recently-desegregated Central High School declared that I was "not college material" and that I would "never get into college," Meachem was one of many who openly wondered, "Why not?" I am forever indebted to him, and I understand now why he would later say that the day I graduated from Harvard was one of the proudest days of his life.

It was also in those early, formative years that I met someone who, for me personally, has been and remains, in my opinion, one of the most influential women in the church. Her name is Lucille Jones. Sister Jones encouraged me to sing while others were intent on having me preach! While I had neither an interest in nor a desire to preach, singing always had its appeal, and I found, under Sister Jones' tutelage, a way to "escape" those who tried to interest me in preaching while still serving God through song. Lucille encouraged me to use the gift that God had given me, and she directed our Children's Choir, though we were careful, even in the 1950s and early 1960s, not to call it a choir. We called it, instead, a "singing group" and I must admit that even to this day I can't tell the difference. But I am thankful for Sister Jones, and I look at her as one of the early pioneers among women in the Church. A woman directing a "singing group" in the Church in those days was, in retrospect, a remarkable feat. She taught me a song called, "I'm Coming Up, Lord" and I have very fond memories of singing that song not only at the local congregation but also at churches in small towns like Okmulgee and Redbird, Oklahoma, where the women, dressed in their "Sunday best" would grab me and hug me and sometimes give me nickels and dimes as I walked back to my seat following my performance! To this very day, Sister Jones and her family remain very close to my family and me, a relationship for which I shall be eternally grateful.

I left Tulsa after graduating from high school and went away to college, then medical school. Attending church services was not a priority for me in those days, and I often think of conversations I had with my uncle Mack whenever I would visit Tulsa. He often chided me for what he called "not taking God to college with (me)." "Did you ask God whether he wanted to go to college?" he would ask. And while I must admit that the question never occurred to me, I found comfort in knowing that not a single day went by when I felt that God was not with me. Not sure that he could understand that, and even less sure that I could possibly explain it to him, my typical response was just to smile and say or do something to change the subject. We both laughed.

After completing a fellowship in neonatal and pediatric anesthesiology in Boston, I took a job at Cedars-Sinai Medical Center in Los Angeles. Cedars-Sinai came to be as a result of a merger of two Jewish hospitals in the area, Cedars of Lebanon and Mount Sinai. Those two hospitals found their genesis in the blatant discrimination that Jewish doctors faced when they tried to obtain privileges at then-existing hospitals in Los Angeles and were denied access. So they built their own: a sprawling campus with a fifteen hundred-bed hospital, each bed in a private room. It was the largest teaching hospital west of the Mississippi River. One of my greatest joys and fondest memories of my thirty plus years at Cedars-Sinai is that I had the privilege of anesthetizing babies so that the Rabbis could perform circumcision on them. My conversations with the Rabbis proved fruitful and educational on many levels, and I thoroughly enjoyed the times we would sit between or following surgeries and just talk. What I came to appreciate most about the Rabbis is that they all knew that I was Christian and, as such, they knew that, despite the fact that we all worshipped the same God, we had fundamental differences in our view of what worship is "supposed" to look like. And yet, not once did any of them ever say, suggest, or even hint that my worship was, in any way, unacceptable to God. Nor did any of them suggest in any way that (as I had heard so many times and for so many years) if I didn't believe what they believed, I would die and go to hell. That was refreshing and was, in fact, the beginning of what I perceive to be a period of tremendous spiritual growth on my part. It ushered in a period in my life when, for the first time, I was not afraid to ask the difficult questions of any text, and I came to realize that no one man has all the right answers.

It was in those years that I found myself growing closer to those who had a similar passion for exploring the riches of God's word and were brave enough to publicly declare what we had learned without fear of being withdrawn from. As I drew closer to sisters, brothers, and even ministers of like mind, it became clear to me that I was growing increasingly uncomfortable with blindly letting others tell me what the Bible said or, more importantly, what it meant. That discomfort lead me to Loyola Marymount University, where I enrolled specifically to study New Testament Greek. I figured that if I could understand not only the meaning of words but also the nuances of the language in which this text was originally written, it would help me to better understand the message the writer intended the original hearers of these letters to grasp. Imagine my surprise and complete dismay when one of the very first things I read in the course text was a sentence that said, "What the student of New Testament Greek needs first and foremost to develop is his (or her) ability to be found wrong." At that point I remember thinking, "If the scholars still get it wrong, is there any hope for me?" And I struggled with that until one day it dawned on me that maybe it's not so much about "right" and "wrong," but it's more about studying God's word and trusting the Holy Spirit to guide you in your beliefs, wherever that might lead and whatever that might look like in practice or in vision.

When one thinks of that word, vision, what typically comes to mind is the idea of perception with the physical organs of sight. Ordinarily, we think of those organs as the eyes. On the contrary, somewhere along this journey, I learned that we look with our eyes but we see with our hearts. My vision, then, for the Church—what I see in my heart—is a place where men and women can come to know what it truly means to be free in Christ. A place where all are encouraged to ask critical questions of the text because, as it has been said, theology often doesn't go from one answer to the next. Instead, it goes from question to a more critical question. A place where every disagreement on matters of interpretation does not become a test of fellowship. A place where men and women, both created in God's image, are free to worship the Lord in whatever capacity they feel the Holy Spirit has guided them. I am convinced that Billy Graham got it right when he said, "If a man accepts the deity of Christ and is living for Christ to the best of his understanding, I intend to have fellowship with him in Christ."

Earlier, I mentioned the conversations I was privileged to have with the Rabbis at the hospital where I have worked for the past 30 plus years. My final vision for the church is one that was actually shaped by one of the Rabbis during a particular conversation I had with him. I was asked one day if I was familiar with the story of the binding of Isaac. Answering in the affirmative, I then listened attentively as the Rabbi offered an explanation of that text from his perspective. "In our tradition," he said, "Isaac represents Judaism." "After all," he continued, "it is only through Isaac that all those promises God made to Abraham could come to fruition. At this point, they had to come through Isaac. If there is no Isaac, there can be no Judaism. So Isaac represents Judaism. Now, when God says to Abraham, 'sacrifice Isaac for me,' what he is really doing is asking Abraham a question and demanding an answer. The question he is asking is, 'Abraham, whom do you love; do you love your God or do you love your religion?' And as Abraham prepared to sacrifice Isaac, he demonstrated that he loved his God more than he loved his religion." My heartfelt prayer and vision for the Church is that it may be so among us. May we, in all that we say and do as the body of Christ, be steadfast in demonstrating that we love our God more than we love our religion.

My Life in the Churches of Christ
by Richard Hughes

I was born into the Church of Christ just as surely as I am alive, and over the years, I have thought that my birth-relation to that church was a little like being born Amish. Mine was a tradition that was all pervasive and all-consuming, and to belong to the Church of Christ meant, by definition, to be separate and other.

We were separate for one simple reason: ours was the one true church since we alone had restored the primitive church described in the biblical text. All the others were cheap imitations, phonies, and frauds, though we used much nicer language to describe them. We called them "the denominations."

I grew up a lot like Danny Saunders in Chaim Potok's novel, *The Chosen*. The son of the Hasidic rabbi, a first generation immigrant to the United States, Danny thrived on mainstream American culture in his newly adopted land, but each afternoon he returned to his profoundly separatist Hasidic world, and the tension he felt between the two was palpable.

Like Danny, my life as a teen was a sheer paradox. I thrived in the public schools in San Angelo, Texas, but my church was a world apart. My parents forbade me to attend the school-sponsored dances or even to learn to dance, for that matter. But they required that our entire family attend Sunday school every Sunday and church three times every week—Sunday morning, Sunday evening, and Wednesday evening. And when the week-long gospel meetings rolled around, as they did twice a year, we were there for every service.

Staying The Course

One story illustrates well the tension I felt between my church and my school—a story that played itself in the context of Texas high school football. If you saw the movie, "Friday Night Lights" starring Billy Bob Thornton, then you will understand at least part of the world in which I grew up, a world in which high school football was king. For every home game, the San Angelo Central High School Bobcats packed the stadium—a magnificent partial bowl built especially for our team—with 11,000 screaming fans, twenty percent of San Angelo's population.

As student body vice-president during my senior year, it fell to me to lead the invocation on one of those nights before the game began. Just before I climbed the stairs to the press box, the student body president caught my arm and offered some advice. "There are many Jews at this game tonight," she said—though looking back, I'm sure she was wrong about that judgment—"and out of respect to them," she continued, "why don't you just end your prayer with a strong 'Amen' and leave off the words, 'In Jesus name?'"

My parents and my church had taught me always to pray "in Jesus' name" since we believed that our prayers reached the Father only through him. But on this particular night and at this particular place, a healthy dose of compromise made good sense to me. So I prayed for the players and I prayed for the fans and I prayed for our country. And when I was finished, I simply said, "Amen."

Two days later, on Sunday morning, several men in our church accosted me. They didn't accost me one by one. They accosted me as a group. They clearly had talked things over among themselves and selected one to speak for the rest. That man got in my face and said, "Boy, that prayer you prayed at that game the other night didn't get no higher than them light poles!"

I felt my face grow hot and red. These men had embarrassed me deeply. I had done what I thought was right in the context of my school, but it turned out to be wrong—profoundly wrong—in the context of my church.

The tension I felt between the world of my school and the world of my church was unrelenting. In spite of the fact that I had found acceptance among my peers, I knew I was "other" and would never be like them.

Mine was—and still is—a profoundly regional church. It has always enjoyed considerable strength in a belt that runs from Tennessee to Texas, but its numbers plummet when one leaves its four-state geographical heartland. But until I was twenty years old, as far as I was concerned, it embodied the whole of Christendom.

And that is why, in the late 1950s, I seriously wondered why the major television networks devoted so much coverage to what the Vatican said about this or that global crisis, but never covered the perspectives of the leading preachers in my church.

Never mind the fact that the Catholic Church was a global church while mine was largely confined to four states in the American Mid-South. And never mind the fact that the Catholic Church had over a billion adherents while mine had maybe a million. If ours was the one true church and therefore the whole of Christendom, I firmly believed that our preachers deserved fully as much coverage as the networks gave the Vatican, and probably even more. Why didn't they interview Batsell Barrett Baxter?

Pointing Me toward a Wider World

But when I was sixteen, my mother said something that began to open my mind to a larger world. A preacher in our tradition had produced a series of filmstrips designed to aid in the task of converting one's friends and neighbors to the one true church. The idea was to invite them in for coffee and dessert and, in that non-threatening environment, to help them see the error of their ways.

When I discovered those filmstrips, I made up my mind to show them to my high school buddies. All my friends belonged to one Christian denomination or another. They were mainly Baptists, Methodists, and Presbyterians. But I didn't consider them genuinely Christian, and I firmly believed they could not be saved so long as they remained outside the one true church. So one day after school, they came to my house to see and hear the great and marvelous truths that I hoped they might embrace.

When I reached the end of my filmstrip presentation, my friends ridiculed me. They thought my perspectives were astoundingly narrow, and that's saying something, considering how narrow all our perspectives were when we were sixteen years old in Texas in the 1950s.

But the most important truth anyone taught that day, however, was imparted neither by the filmstrips nor by me nor by my friends, but by my mother, for once my friends had left our house, my mother spoke words that have shaped my thinking—and, indeed, my life—in profoundly far-reaching ways.

"Son," she said, "if you want to convert your friends to our church, that is entirely up to you. But if you discover that they are right and you are wrong, then you must be the one who is willing to make the change."

As I reflect on those words my mother spoke over half a century ago, I realize that she gave me that day one of the greatest gifts a mother can give a child, short of life itself and a mother's love. The gift was the charge to see the world through someone else's eyes.

My mother's words placed a dent in my true-church armor, but that armor began to crack in serious ways during my years at Harding College. One day a college friend told me something that I had never grasped before—that our church was essentially confined to four southern states—Tennessee, Arkansas, Oklahoma, and Texas. As insular as I was, it somehow made no sense to me that all God's children—all the saved from throughout the earth—were essentially confined to four states in the American South.

In addition, some of my professors did their best to open my mind—and the minds of my peers—to the possibility of a wider world than the one I had imagined.

For example, I first encountered religions other than the Christian religion in a world literature textbook that contained selections from the Koran and the Bhagavad Gita. I knew there were people who claimed to be Christian but whose claims were patently false since they didn't belong to the one true church. I found that fact troubling enough. But before reading those selections from the Gita and the Koran, I had never given the slightest thought to the fact that millions of people in the world embrace religions other than Christianity.

Making that discovery shook me to the core, for it forced me to ask if the fact that I was a Christian—indeed, if the fact that I belonged to the one true church—was more the result of having been born into a "true-church" family and a nation that was nominally Christian than anything else.

That question troubled me so profoundly that I went to my professor to seek his counsel and advice. He told me that I should neither run from the question nor bury it, but to face it head-on and carefully work through its implications. He told me that if I faced the question with honesty and candor, I would reach an appropriate answer, but he refused to tell me what an appropriate answer might be.

More than anything else, those sorts of experiences drove me toward what would become my vocation. I knew I could never understand myself until I understood the Churches of Christ—the Christian tradition that had raised me. By now, I had begun to suspect that the origins of Churches of Christ were far more complicated than the simple claim that we had sprung full-blown from the biblical text. It now seemed clear to me that our church had a history far more complex than that. But what was that history? What were our roots? And what were the cultural and religious forces that had produced this tradition? Those questions tugged at my heart and mind with such urgency that I decided to devote my life to finding some answers. I would become a church historian.

Abilene Christian College

My first stop on that journey was Abilene Christian College, where I enrolled in an M.A. program in Christian history and began to make some startling discoveries about Churches of Christ. I learned, for example, that Alexander Campbell, shaped as he was by the Age of Reason, had taught us to read the Bible through the lens of modern science. The Bible, he often said, was a book of facts that offered clear instructions on how to do church.

That discovery shook my complacent assumption that we in Churches of Christ had never interpreted the Bible, had never read it through a cultural lens, but simply took it for what it was and read it as it was meant to be read. It also helped me grasp why we were so focused on questions of form and structure.

And then, in the midst of these startling discoveries, one of my professors at ACC—the eminent patristics scholar, Dr. Everett Ferguson—placed in my hands a book that would turn my world upside down.

That book told the story of Swiss Christians who lived in the sixteenth century, more than four hundred years before my time, but who, like Churches of Christ, committed themselves to restore the true and ancient church

But as I read that book, I discovered a radical difference between their agenda and ours, a difference that challenged all my assumptions about the meaning of the Christian faith. In our concern with the forms and structures of the ancient church, we sought to recover the true form of worship, the correct plan of salvation, the right form of baptism, and the proper organization of the church. We asked how often the Lord's Supper should be celebrated, and some of us even asked whether we should use one cup or many. Out of the entire Bible, our one special text was the book of Acts since Acts was the book that most fully revealed what we perceived as the pattern of the primitive church.

In fact, so committed were we to the book of Acts as a seminal text that when I was ten years old, my mother refused to let me play ball with my friends during those blissful summer months until I had memorized each day significant chunks of that text.

But now I was reading about a band of Swiss Christians over four hundred years ago who committed themselves as did we to the task of restoration, but who seldom focused on the Book of Acts. Instead, they focused on the Gospels. And they seldom asked the question, "What were the forms and structures of the primitive church that should now be restored?" Instead, they asked, "What does it mean to be a disciple of Jesus?"

The book that opened to me this whole new world was Franklin H. Littell's classic study, *The Anabaptist View of the Church*. Each page was for me a revelation that often left me stunned in near disbelief. How could a group of Christians who aimed to restore the primitive church embrace an agenda this different from the one I had been taught? For example, here were Christians who placed at the center of the Christian faith Jesus' command to feed the hungry, clothe and naked, and care for "the least of these." And while the political and religious leaders of sixteenth-century Europe murdered these people by the thousands, Jesus' command to "love your enemies" was for them the heart and soul of the task of restoration. They, therefore, refused to take up the sword, even when others took up the sword against them.

I found the Anabaptist vision so biblical and so compelling that for my M.A. thesis, I compared the restoration ideals of the sixteenth-century Anabaptists with the restoration ideals of my own tradition. That project radically transformed my understanding of the Christian faith, my assessment of the restoration ideal, and my appraisal of my own tradition, the Churches of Christ.

The University of Iowa

My encounter with the sixteenth-century Anabaptists could not have come at a more propitious time, for it prepared me for the intellectual and emotional earthquake that would rattle my world when I enrolled in a doctoral program at the University of Iowa in the fall of 1967.

My experience there breathed new life into the charge my mother gave me when I was only sixteen—the charge to see the world through the eyes of others. At Iowa, those others were American Blacks and Vietnamese on the other side of the world.

It was 1967, after all. The Civil Rights Movement challenged the racist structures of American life, and the anti-war movement rejected the nation's military venture in Vietnam. Universities throughout the country were awash with questions of social justice. At Iowa, thoughtful debates over race and war became my daily bread. I could not have escaped those issues, even had I tried. My professors raised them, my fellow students raised them, and I found at Iowa—especially in its School of Religion—a community bathed in a sea of moral and ethical passion.

Before I left the South for my doctoral studies at Iowa, some in the Church of Christ warned me that if I pursued doctoral studies at a place like the University of Iowa—a state school north of the Mason-Dixon Line—I would doubtless lose my faith.

In one respect, they were right. The moral climate at Iowa stripped me of comforting orthodoxies and narrow provincial assumptions. In their place, this "godless" state institution helped me develop a faith that was far more robust, far more reflective, and far more nuanced. The biblical perspective of the Anabaptists helped me make sense of the world I encountered at Iowa, and I began to develop an ethical compass I had never known before—a compass informed both by the Christian faith and by people whose view of the world was very different from my own.

The question of racial justice was a case in point. Even though I attended college in the American South from 1961 to 1965, just a few hundred miles from many of the greatest struggles of the Freedom Movement—the 1963 Children's March in Birmingham, for example, or the attempted march across the Edmund Pettus Bridge in Selma, Alabama, on Bloody Sunday in 1964—I sailed through college life, blissfully unaware of the great moral struggles that defined those years, and today, sadly, have no first-hand memory of any of those events.

Malcolm X was murdered on my birthday, February 21, during my senior year in college, 1965. I'm not sure I even knew who Malcolm was. But Iowa forced me to reckon with people like Malcolm and Martin and the values for which they stood.

I served at Iowa as a teaching assistant in a large undergraduate course titled, "Religion in Human Culture." One of the books students read for that course was Alex Haley's *Autobiography of Malcolm X*.[1] Malcolm's life was a revelation to me in more ways than one. Having had no experience with urban blacks, I didn't know people like Malcolm even existed. Malcolm taught me—for the very first time—the meaning of systemic racism and helped me to grasp what it meant to be poor and black in America's inner cities. Slowly, I began to see why Malcolm viewed whites as devils, why he turned his back on Christianity as a tool of white oppressors, and why he found Islam so attractive.

---

[1] Alex Haley, *The Autobiography of Malcolm X* (Grove Press, 1966).

My rigorous engagement with Malcolm X typified my Iowa experience. In geographical distance, Iowa was not all that far from my home—less than a thousand miles, almost due north. But in other respects, it might well have been a million miles away or even on the moon.

Diamonds in My Own Backyard

A few years later, however, I would discover that neither the University of Iowa nor those Anabaptists of the sixteenth century were as far from my roots as I had imagined.

Both required me to open my mind to a larger, more expansive search for truth. But when in 1981 I began to write my history of Churches of Christ—the book I called *Reviving the Ancient Faith*—I discovered that a rigorous search for truth stood at the heart of my own tradition. The earliest leaders of my church—people like Alexander Campbell (1788-1866), for example—made critical thinking and the constant search for truth central to living out the fullness of the Christian faith, though that was a virtue I seldom encountered in the churches of my youth.

And while both Iowa and the Anabaptists forced me to deal with questions of social justice, I discovered in my own Christian tradition people who thought that social justice was central to biblical faith and to the task of restoration. Those people seldom used the term, social justice. Instead, they used the phrase that Jesus so often used—"the kingdom of God."

That phrase—"the kingdom of God"—shows up in the New Testament well over 100 times, and the frequency with which it appears should tell us that "the kingdom of God" is a key component of the Christian faith. To learn what it means, we need only consult the various contexts that surround the verses where that phrase appears.

If we take the trouble to do that work, we will quickly learn that the biblical vision of the kingdom of God embodies two ideas that were close to the heart of Jesus—(1) peacemaking ("love your enemies") and (2) Jesus' commitment to care for those he called "the least of these"—the poor, the hungry, the naked, the stranger, the homeless, the oppressed, and those in prison.

Those are themes that defined the thinking of people like Barton W. Stone and David Lipscomb. But Churches of Christ, for a variety of reasons, turned their collective backs on those ideals during and after World War I. By the time I came of age, preachers in my church seldom or never spoke of Jesus' vision of the kingdom of God, and no one could remember when they did. Instead, they presented the gospel in terms of forms and structures that appealed chiefly to the rational mind.

But the rigorous search for truth, on the one hand, and the kingdom of God, on the other, are crucial themes that Churches of Christ, if we are still serious about biblical faith, should zealously work to recover.

To my mind, no preacher in American history articulated the biblical vision of the kingdom of God with greater power than Martin Luther King Jr. And I have found no single text that offers us greater encouragement to see the world through the eyes of others than King's prophetic words when he spoke against America's involvement in the Vietnam War at New York's famed Riverside Church in 1967—a speech that likely hastened his death.

On that occasion, he urged the American people "to see the enemy's point of view, to hear his questions, to know his assessment of ourselves. For from his view," he argued, "we may indeed see the basic weaknesses of our own condition, and if we are mature, we may learn and grow and profit from the wisdom of the brothers who are called the opposition."[2]

Somehow I believe that my mother was pointing me toward that sort of vision when she told me during my sixteenth year, "If you discover that they are right and you are wrong, then you must be the one who is willing to make the change."

---

[2] Martin Luther King Jr., "A Time to Break Silence" [1967], in *A Testament of Hope: The Essential Writings and Speeches of Martin Luther King Jr.*, ed. James Melvin Washington (San Francisco: HarperSanFrancisco, 1986), p. 237.

Crossroads: A Personal Journey by Jack Scott

Robert Frost's famous poem "The Road Not Taken" begins with the line, "Two roads diverged in a yellow road." He then writes that he took the less traveled one. He describes his subsequent journey as "way leads on to way."

As I reflect upon my own life, certainly way has led on to way. And that journey has been marked by crucial crossroads along the way. In this autobiographical tale, I have chosen to focus on seven crossroads in my life.

I was born and raised in Sweetwater, Texas, a small West Texas town of 10,000 people. I was very blessed to have loving and nurturing parents. Among my earliest memories was time spent at the 4th and Elm Street Church of Christ in my hometown. Here my father was an elder and my mother was a Sunday School teacher. We were there when the church doors opened: Sunday morning, Sunday night, and Wednesday night.

My childhood was focused on family, church, and school. It was shortly after my high school graduation that I faced my first important crossroad, "What shall I do with my life?" After some thought, I decided to be a minister. With this clear sense of commitment, I entered Abilene Christian College and majored in Bible.

My four years at ACC were most enjoyable and rewarding. I preached regularly at rural churches near Abilene, which was customary for preacher students in those days. I have often marveled at the patience of those good country people, who listened to an eighteen-year-old expound upon the Scriptures. I was on the debate team and was elected president of the student body; these experiences gave me speaking experience and leadership development. But, most important, Abilene Christian College is the place where I met my future wife, Lacreta. We were married shortly after my graduation in 1954.

The second important crossroad in my life occurred in 1957. At that time, I was Director of Alumni Relations at ACC; I also continued to preach on Sundays. During an interim stint at the Birdville Church of Christ in Fort Worth, an elder mentioned to me that they would be interested in sponsoring me in mission work if I desired to do so.

This encouragement led me to consider two goals in my life: to preach outside the Bible Belt (i.e., Church of Christ land) and to pursue graduate study in religion. So in the fall of 1957, Lacreta and I, with two young daughters, left Abilene to move to New Haven, Connecticut. When I arrived, the church there had about 25 members and was meeting in a rented hall. For the first two years, I spent all my time as a minister. We were blessed to build a building with help from Texas churches and to grow to about 80 members. Then in 1959, I enrolled in Yale Divinity School.

Let me describe my faith at that time. I thoroughly believed and preached the doctrines of the Church of Christ. I had been warned against the liberalism of seminaries such as Yale, and I was fully prepared to resist their teachings.

However, slowly, there began to be changes in some of my beliefs. For one thing, I became more ecumenical. I recall being struck by the life of Francis of Assisi. This young man gave up all of his possessions and identified with lepers and other outcasts of society. He seemed to be more of a true disciple of Jesus than some of my brethren. Was he to be denied heaven because he was not a member of the Church of Christ?

Furthermore, I began to realize that I could hold to Biblical truths without having to defend the accuracy of the scientific and cultural framework in which these words were written. For example, I need not argue about the age of the earth. Another example is that I could accept the story of the Tower of Babel as teaching the folly of the human pride without looking to it as the scientific explanation of the origin of language.

As I was concluding my Master of Divinity degree at Yale in 1962, I came to the third major crossroad of my life. For many years, my dream had been to teach religion in one of our Christian colleges. I was fortunate to receive an offer from Pepperdine College to join their religion faculty. So in August of 1962, my wife and I packed up all our belongings, put them in a large trailer behind our car, and, along with three small daughters, made the 3,000-mile trek to Los Angeles.

The ten years (1962-72) we spent at Pepperdine were rich and rewarding. We made lifelong friends among fellow faculty members and their families. Through a Danforth Teachers Grant, I was able to complete my Ph.D. in History at Claremont Graduate University with an emphasis upon American religious history. Also during that time, I continued to preach regularly at Los Angeles area churches.

A particularly rich experience was serving as the minister for the Crenshaw Church of Christ, a church that was founded on the intention of integrating white and African American Christians. Having been raised in a segregated town, it early became a passion of mine to speak against racial injustice.

It was also during this time that I began my administrative career, serving as a dean and later as Provost of the Los Angeles campus at Pepperdine. In fact, I began to realize that college administration was my calling and believed that this was my best avenue of service. But I also slowly reached the conclusion that I would leave Pepperdine, which constituted the fourth crossroad of my life.

Let me explain the reason. For many years the movement of some of our colleges toward identification with Republican politics disturbed me. As a student of the Restoration movement, I knew this was not characteristic of the earlier days of the Church of Christ. Leaders such as David Lipscomb and J.N. Armstrong, founding president of Harding College, strongly advocated the separation of church from politics. But a later president of Harding College, Dr. George Benson, went in the opposite direction. In the 1940s, Benson advocated conservative political views and successfully received considerable contributions as a result. Other Christian colleges such as Pepperdine eventually followed this path. In fact, *Wikipedia* identifies Pepperdine University as not only a Christian college but also as prominent "as one of the United States' leading centers of conservative politics, attracting many conservative-leaning professors." I realized my administrative effectiveness at Pepperdine would be hindered by my hesitance to embrace conservative causes.

Bill Banowsky, former President of Pepperdine, in his book *The Malibu Miracle*, confirmed my recognition of this difficulty. He spoke highly of my administrative skills and integrity, but he stated that my "moderately Democratic but deeply held political convictions would not keep time with Pepperdine Republican priorities." He added that Pepperdine potential demanded "doctrinal conservatism in religion and politics."

Rather than consign myself to a minority voice at Pepperdine, I chose to leave. For the first time in my adult life, I was no longer employed by any segment of the Church of Christ. This separation was painful, but I believed it to be necessary.

On January 1, 1973, I accepted a position as the chief academic officer at Orange Coast College in Costa Mesa. Thus began my 23-year career in California community colleges. Later I became President of Cypress College (1978-87) and then President of Pasadena City College (1987-95). These years were most fruitful and meaningful. I was able to improve these colleges through academic programs and to initiate building construction. I felt spiritually fulfilled in improving the lives of thousands of community college students. Many of these students were low-income; many were also the first in their family to attend college. Also, community colleges mirrored the ethnic diversity of California, serving thousands of students of color. I continued to preach during this period on a once-a-month engagement at the Sierra Madre Church of Christ.

The fifth crossroad of my life was not one of my own choosing. On October 23, 1993, a deputy sheriff knocked on our door to inform us that our son, Adam, had been shot and killed. He was attending a dinner party when the host of the party displayed a gun. A shot was fired and Adam was dead. Adam was the youngest of our five children. He graduated with a law degree from the University of Southern California just a few months before his death. He was employed by a Los Angeles law firm. Notification of his passing the bar and his business cards arrived at our home after he was killed.

How does one recover from such a tragedy? On the day of Adam's death, George Regas, a friend and rector of All Saints Church in Pasadena, came to visit us. I asked him, "George, how will I ever get over this?" He truthfully answered, "You won't. You will always walk with a limp. But you can go through life with a limp."

Fortunately, our faith was not dependent on facile answers. Several months before this event, I had preached a sermon titled *'What About Naboth?'* You recall that Naboth was the innocent victim of Ahab and Jezebel's greed for Naboth's vineyard. They conspired to have him falsely accused, and Naboth was executed. And although Ahab and Jezebel were subsequently punished, Naboth was still dead. Yes, bad things happen to good people. As the book of Job teaches, we can only trust in God when we don't have a complete answer in the face of tragedy.

So with God's help, the support of wonderful friends, and grief counseling, we did manage to move on. We were counseled to turn our grief into positive action when possible. So Lacreta gave herself to her students at Cerritos College, where she was an English professor. Shortly after Adam's death, George Regas and I founded an organization in Pasadena, the Coalition for a Non-Violent City. Also, on several occasions, Lacreta and I have comforted and counseled parents who have lost children. We have tried to use our experience of sorrow to serve others.

And I now come to the sixth crossroad of my life. This crossroad was, frankly, an unexpected turn. It was in October 1995. I was planning to retire from Pasadena City College to accept an offer from Pepperdine University to be a Distinguished Professor of Higher Education. This seemed like an appropriate conclusion to my academic career; I could share my experience and thoughts with graduate students in education.

But then a group of citizens came to me to ask me to run for office. They believed that someone of my reputation in the community could be elected to the California Assembly. The incumbent was a right-wing

Republican, who had not served the community well and had made some questionable ethical decisions.

My first response was, "No," but I promised to consider it. After Lacreta and I discussed it, and I consulted with my children and some close friends, I decided to take the plunge. One might ask, "Why would a Christian enter the dirty world of politics?" Of course, one might answer that if good people refuse to enter politics, to whom do we leave our government?

So I decided to run, knowing that it would be tough and, at times, ugly. Politics is a contact sport. But after a long, hard campaign, I won by nine percentage points. In my subsequent elections, I was fortunate to win by a larger percentage each time.

I served four years in the State Assembly (1996-2000) and eight years in the State Senate (2000-2008). During that time, I authored 146 bills that were signed into law. I was particularly involved in educational issues since that was my background. I also authored bills on gun safety; my own tragedy made my voice particularly powerful on that issue. On some occasions, I spoke for those who could not speak for themselves, such as opening the armories on occasions to house the homeless. The motto I tried to follow was that well-known passage in Micah that enunciates God's requirement of man: "to do justice; to love mercy; and to walk humbly with your God."

Was it difficult to remain independent in making decisions? Of course. I often recalled the sage advice of my ethics professor at Yale, James Gustafson. In relation to institutions, he warned, "Always ride loose in the saddle." But overall, my twelve years in the state legislature was a great experience. I was able to make some outstanding friends. On occasions, I was asked to speak in churches, particularly African-American churches.

And after completing my term in the Senate, I was asked to be the Chancellor of California Community Colleges. It was a large responsibility, overseeing 112 colleges and 2.1 million students. But after this service, I came to the seventh crossroad of my life, the decision to retire.

After completing 58 years of full-time employment, I believed it was time to slow down and simply choose a few things that I still enjoy doing. Now I am a Scholar-in-Residence at Claremont Graduate University, where I occasionally teach a class. I also lecture on occasions and consult. I preach on a bi-monthly basis at the Sierra Madre Church of Christ and have taught a couple of classes at lectureships. And I find I have more time for family and friends.

As I reflect on my life, I believe I have been incredibly blessed. My life with Lacreta for over 61 years has been rich and wonderful. We still have four fine children (Sharon Mitchell, Sheila Head, Amy Schones, and Greg Scott) and eleven grandchildren. I can look back and view each portion of my life as a ministry and a calling. I have made mistakes and certainly possess flaws. Yet I am confident of God's gracious forgiveness to cover these sins. As the Psalmist wrote, I thank God and say, "You anoint my head with oil; my cup runs over."

A Hopeful Future for the Churches of Christ

Now that I have shared my journey of faith, permit me also to share a few recommendations that I would suggest for the Churches of Christ. Having been raised in the Church of Christ and having spent eight decades in this body, it is my family. So I offer these suggestions out of love, not in a spirit of harsh criticism.

Furthermore, I freely admit my fallibility. In I Corinthians 13:12, Paul writes, "Now we see in a mirror, dimly." So allow me to use my dim mirror of knowledge to make these observations.

In my youth, the Churches of Christ were growing rapidly. Not so today. *The Christian Chronicle* recently reported that since 1980, our membership the United States has declined from 1,240,820 to 1,183,613—a loss of 57,207 members. What accounts for this decrease, and are there steps we might take to reverse this trend? Here are four concrete recommendations.

1. Re-examine our stance on the women's issue. With some exception, today most Churches of Christ do not permit women to pray publicly, preside at the Lord's Supper, or preach. A young woman in my own congregation who grew up in the church and gave much to the church has left because she is so offended at our not

using women in public worship.

We live in a culture where women are in all occupations, often in leading roles. In a recent conversation with my granddaughter, a professional woman, she commented that if corporations practiced gender discrimination as some churches do, it would be illegal.

Women prayed and prophesied in the early church (Acts 21:9; I Corinthians 11:5). The basic principle is well stated by Paul in Galatians 3:28, "There is neither Jew nor Greek, there is neither slave nor free, there is neither male nor female; for we are all one in Christ." To continue a male-dominated worship service is a significant barrier to many men and women and will deny the church the very meaningful contribution that women can make.

2. Adopt a kinder attitude toward Christians in other churches. One of the mottoes of the early Restoration Movement was, "We are not the only Christians, but we are Christians only." In 1837, a woman criticized Alexander Campbell for referring to Methodists as Christians. He replied to her, "Who is a Christian? Everyone that believes in his heart that Jesus of Nazareth is the Messiah, the Son of God, repents of his sins, and obeys him in all things according to his knowledge." Campbell made it clear that he believed in immersion, but also made it clear that a Christian did not have to be perfect in all things.

Too often, we in the Churches of Christ have been viewed as believing we are the only Christians. We have approached members of other churches with a superior attitude of "I am right, and you are wrong." This attitude is obviously counter-productive and deeply offends others.

3. Re-examine our interpretation of the New Testament. In our search for a pattern for the church, we have placed too much emphasis on minor details rather than principles. Sadly, this legalistic approach has produced divisions in our ranks. Today there are four splits from the "mainline" Church of Christ, based on one cup for the communion, non-Sunday School, non-located preacher, and non-cooperation. Jesus often attacked the scribes and

Pharisees for their legalistic approach to the law. Of them, he said, "You pay tithe of mint, anise, and cumin, and have neglected the weightier matters of the law; justice and mercy and faith" (Matthew 23:23).

In searching the New Testament for rules, not only have we been inconsistent, but also we have conveniently not required some practices of the early church such as fasting (Acts 13:2,3), elders anointing the sick with oil (James 5:14), and women's head being covered in worship (I Corinthians 11:5). For instance, I have heard serious arguments over how many children an elder must have rather than emphasizing the qualities elders should have as outlined in I Timothy and Titus.

The point is that unity does not require unanimity. As long as we are imperfect in our knowledge and life, we will sometimes disagree. But this normally should not lead to division. To do so is lacking in Christian love and is a poor example to those outside the church.

4. Restore the spirit of New Testament Christianity. In Jesus' vivid description of the final judgment (Matthew 25-31-46), he separated people on the basis of their love for others. He praised those who fed the hungry, clothed the naked, gave drink to the thirsty, and visited the sick and those in prison. He condemned those who had failed to do those things. Following Jesus' teachings, the early disciples were noted for their care for the poor.

5. Some of our churches have been outstanding in this regard. I know of a small church in Honduras which decided to feed lunches to schoolchildren in their town; most of these children came from homes in deep poverty. Soon their congregation doubled in size. The African Christian Hospitals in Nigeria, Ghana, and Tanzania sponsor seven medical clinics that treat thousands of patients every year. Not surprisingly, the Church of Christ is growing rapidly in these parts of Africa.

Wouldn't it be wonderful if the Churches of Christ became known for their love? The restoration of New Testament Christianity is not merely reproducing its form. To merely reproduce the form is to create a museum piece. Rather we must embody the love of Jesus, who loved the lepers, the mentally ill, and the poor. Jesus enjoined us to love our neighbor as ourselves.

Many other suggestions could be made; however, I believe these four recommendations are worthy of consideration. Following these recommendation does call for change, and change is always difficult. Yet Jesus called for change in first century Palestine, and he calls for change today. After all, the first-century church had to make a dramatic transformation when they moved from a Jewish-only institution to a universal church.

Furthermore, I believe the recommendations outlined in this paper will make the message of the New Testament even more appealing. Growth will take care of itself. And we as Churches of Christ can more nearly fulfill that prayer of Jesus: "Your kingdom come: your will be done, on earth as it is in heaven."

Memoirs and Vision
by Fred D. Gray

Introduction

I am honored to have been invited by Gayle Crowe to be one of the Presenters at this "Memoirs and Visions" session of the June Scholars Conference 2018, Lipscomb University in Nashville, TN. Thanks to my good friend David Fleer who I am sure planted the seed in the mind of Mr. Crowe for my participation today.

Thanks also to President L. Randolph Lowry and Lipscomb University. They have played a major role, also, in me receiving the invitation to speak to you today. On April 20, 2016, after some negotiating over a 5-year period of time, a Memorandum of Understanding ("MOU") was executed between Lipscomb University, by its President, Dr. Lowry, and by me, Fred D. Gray. A portion of the introductory paragraph to the MOU states that…

> …the MOU "will serve as a statement of our mutual intent to work together and set out a path that Lipscomb University ("Lipscomb") and Fred D. Gray ("Gray") can embrace for a productive and long-lasting relationship. For the benefit of future generations, Gray and Lipscomb desire to memorialize their previous correspondence and numerous discussions related to education focused on racial reconciliation, equality, and justice, which the parties have referred to in said correspondence as the "Fred Gray Initiative" (the "Initiative"). The Initiative seeks to honor the legacy of Gray by keeping alive his career work to "destroy everything segregated" and

embolden his vision for a just and equitable society through six substantial streams, including an agreement that the board of directors of the Christian Scholars Conference would name a lecture, the "Fred D. Gray Lecture."

Therefore, I am appreciative to many persons for the honor bestowed upon me; naming one of the lectures of this conference after me, and for me to be able to share with you today by "Memoirs and Vision." I have been asked to speak to you about my "memoirs – citing people, places, and events that led you to become the spiritually-focused leader you are." Then, I was asked to conclude by painting a picture of the "vision" for what I "think the Restoration Movement/Stone-Campbell Movement/Churches of Christ might evolve into over the next few decades."

It will be relatively easy for me to share with you my memoirs. You can determine what, if anything, I have been able to contribute to the church, to the nation, to the world in whatever field. It may or may not be a little more difficult to share with you my "vision" of where the church should be during the next few years ahead.

Memoirs

My Early Life

I was born on December 14, 1930, in Montgomery, Alabama. My mother was Nancy Jones Gray Arms (August 19, 1894-October 3, 1992) and my father was Abraham Gray (July 15, 1874-December 23, 1932). Mom worked as a domestic, particularly a cook, in several white homes in Montgomery. My father was a carpenter who received his training at Tuskegee Institute. He died when I was two. After his death, mom taught us that we could be whatever we wanted to be if we did three things: (1) keep Christ first in our lives; (2) stay in school and get a good education and (3) stay out of trouble. I think we did all three.

I was born in a shotgun house at 135 Hercules Street in the Washington Park section of Montgomery. A shotgun house was one with all of the rooms built directly behind each other. It probably was so called because if a person fired a shotgun through the front door, the shot would travel through each of the rooms and out the back door. In 1930, Washington Park was a typical black community in Montgomery, with no paved streets, no running water, and no inside sanitary facilities. There were no hospitals for African-American children to be born. They, like me, were delivered by a midwife.

My parents were members of the Holt Street Church of Christ, located at 975 South Holt Street. My father became a member in 1925 and my mother in 1928. Religion and the church played a major role in my life. My father was a faithful member until his death. He helped to build the first church building. He would canvass our neighborhood and take all the children to Sunday school. After his death, Mom would take us to Sunday school and church. The church was the center of our childhood and our life. Each of us became members of the church at an early age. That church played a major role in my life, the lives of all my brothers and sister, and in the lives of many other African Americans in central Alabama.

My sister Pearl (September 1924-June 2011) recognized the important role the church played in our lives. In 1997, she wrote a book on the history of that church, *The History of the Holt Street Church of Christ and its Role in Establishing Churches of Christ Among African Americans in Central Alabama.* My other siblings are Hassan, Thomas, and Hugh. They are all deceased.

My Early Church Life

The first preacher I recall was Bro. William Whittaker. He was a very good preacher. I was very interested in being a preacher. At an early age, I used to say I wanted to be a gospel preacher just like Bro. Whittaker. I wasn't able to pronounce "gospel" very well. I am told that I baptized cats, dogs, and anything else I could get my hand on. Over the years, my mother always wanted me to be a preacher.

The second preacher I remember was Bro. Sutton Johnson, who was from Tennessee. He told my mother, the officials, and others at the church about a Church of Christ boarding school in Nashville, Tennessee, called the Nashville Christian Institute (NCI). He thought I should attend. Based on his recommendation and with the assistance of the church, in 1943, Bro. Johnson took Robert McBride, another young boy from Holt Street whose father was one of the Elders, and me in his car to Nashville, TN. The school was operated by members of the Church of Christ.

The Bible was taught daily by members of the Church of Christ, along with chapel services. Emphasis was placed on teaching young men to become preachers and church leaders.

From my childhood, mom wanted me to pursue the ministry. This school became part of her plan.

My Life at NCI

NCI was a small, grades 1-12, boarding school. We had approximately three hundred students from about twenty-five states. Our facilities were meager, but we had dedicated faculty members who were genuinely interested in the growth and development of its students. They gave us a good college preparatory education, and many of the graduates of NCI have been and are leaders across the country and preachers in Churches of Christ throughout the nation. Many of the students who attended NCI later attended Southwestern Christian College and became outstanding citizens in their communities, engaged in various businesses and professions across the country, in addition to being ministers and church leaders.

During my stay at NCI, we all developed very close ties and friendships that have lasted a lifetime. When I arrived at the Nashville Christian Institute, I met Robert Woods, who retired as minister of the Monroe Street Church of Christ in Chicago, Illinois. He retired in Villa Rica, Georgia, and died in 2017. Later Obie Elie became my classmate. We were best friends until his death in 2008. He was an outstanding businessman in Cleveland, Ohio.

When Bro. Marshall Keeble became President of NCI, I was selected as one of the boy preachers who traveled with him across the country, recruiting students and raising funds for NCI. I learned a great deal from him about the church and about how to live. I graduated in 1948.

Fred D. Gray

A Student at Alabama State College, 1947-1951

I enrolled in Alabama State College for Negroes, now Alabama State University, on December 1, 1947. All my life I had been drawn to the ministry and when I entered Alabama State, I envisioned becoming a social science teacher and a minister, as those were the principal careers then open to college-educated African-American males. You either preached or taught school. But my studies and associations at Alabama State began to change my goals.

Professor Thelma Glass taught history, geography, and English. She impressed upon her students the recipe for success in college. She advised us to learn exactly what the professor wanted, how the professor wanted the material presented, and then to try to present it in that fashion. I have followed this advice ever since, not only in college, but in law school and law practice.

Another professor who made an indelible impression on me was J. E. Pierce, who taught political science and had done an extensive survey in the area of voter registration. Professor Pierce often talked about the importance of obtaining our civil rights. He noted my interest in civil rights and encouraged me to go to law school.

I worked my way through Alabama State College as a district manager of the Alabama Journal, the then afternoon daily paper in Montgomery. I was known on campus as the "newspaper boy." My delivery territory, District Six, encompassed the campus and all of the east side of Montgomery where African-Americans resided—African-American district managers supervised African-American areas, and white district managers supervised white areas. As a district manager, it was my responsibility to oversee the distribution of the newspaper for thirteen routes, to employ and manage newspaper carriers, and to increase circulation.

Although it seems that I was always working, always getting on and off the buses, my grades never suffered. I graduated with honors in the upper 10 percent of my class.

Private Pledge to Destroy Segregation

By my junior year, I understood more fully that everything was completely segregated not only in Montgomery but throughout the South and in many places across the nation. In Alabama's capital city—the "Birthplace of the Confederacy"—churches, schools, hospitals, and places of public accommodation were all segregated. Whites and blacks were segregated from the time they were born until the time they were buried in segregated cemeteries. If a person of color had a claim against a white person, there was very little likelihood he would obtain justice. There were no African American lawyers in Montgomery at that time. Very few white lawyers would handle these cases. I concluded that in addition to being a minister and trying to save souls for eternity, that in the here and now African Americans were entitled to all the rights provided by the Constitution of the United States of America. Therefore, I decided I would become a lawyer. Privately, I pledged that I would return to Montgomery and use the law to "destroy everything segregated I could find." I kept my plans secret. I did not want anything to interfere with me obtaining my goal.

Selection of a Law School

In my senior year, I applied to several law schools, including Western Reserve University, now Case Western Reserve University in Cleveland. I selected schools in cities where job opportunities existed. As far as I could discern, Cleveland was a good place to both learn law and get a job. Another influential factor was Case Western Reserve University's schedule of classes. I could take classes from 8:30 in the morning until 12:30 in the afternoon and still have time to work a part-time job and study.

After I was admitted, I showed my mother my acceptance letter. She said, "All right, Mr. Smarty, now that you have been admitted where are you going to get the money from?" She told me to "never stop preaching," and I have not.

I did not apply to the University of Alabama Law School because I knew I would not be accepted. The State of Alabama, as did all of the southern states at that time, had out-of-state aid arrangements for African American students who on their merits should have been admitted to white colleges, universities and professional schools. Many southern states inaugurated these schemes to comply with the 1938 United States Supreme Court decision, *Gaines v. Canada, ex rel.* The *Gaines* case held that states that had a segregated higher education system must provide African Americans with equal educational facilities. I took advantage of this program.

On one of the last few days of my employment at the Advertiser Company, one of the white district managers asked me what I was going to do after graduation. I told him I was going to law school. Another district manager asked me, "Well, where are you going to practice law?" I said, "Right across the street." There was a long silence. The Montgomery County Courthouse at that time was located across the street from the Advertiser Company.

A Law Student At Western Reserve University, 1951-1954

In September of 1951, with barely enough money to cover travel expenses, I took a segregated train from Montgomery to Cleveland to begin law studies at Western Reserve University. I was assigned housing at 1408 Bell Flower Road, known as the Hudson House. Western Reserve had several houses, each with its own housemother. I was on the second floor, and my roommate was Pohlmann Bracewell, from Monrovia, Liberia, West Africa.

Of the approximately 120 students in my class, five were African-Americans. There were seven upper-class African American students. All of us became lawyers. One of them, Edwin L. Davis, became my law partner and helped with many of my civil rights cases. He died in Montgomery.

From day one at Western Reserve, I reminded myself constantly that I would return to Alabama to practice. I began to prepare to return to Alabama. I knew that the most difficult part of the Alabama law that differed from the general law of the other states was in the area of pleadings and practice. Title Seven of the Alabama Code was that part of the statute that I had to master. I purchased a copy, and in my spare time, I typed and outlined that entire title of the Alabama Code.

Professor Samuel Sonnenfield, my faculty advisor, taught me something that has been one of the guiding principles of my law practice. He advised me always to seek assistance and never be afraid to share a fee with an older lawyer who has more experience. I really took that advice to heart. In all of my early cases, including the civil rights cases, I always involved some other experienced lawyer. Those other local African-American lawyers were usually Arthur Shores, sometimes Orzell Billingsley and Peter Hall, all of Birmingham and Charles Langford of Montgomery, who later became one of my law partners. The white lawyer upon whom I depended most for advice was Clifford Durr.

My first year of law school was very difficult. I had to prove to myself that I could do the work. I had an inferiority complex about having graduated from Alabama State College for Negroes. All of the professors and teachers were white. I had never lived in a white environment. In fact, virtually everything around Reserve was white. I was under a lot of self-imposed pressure. Many of the white students had done their undergraduate work at Harvard, Yale, Princeton, and Western Reserve universities. I was anxious to see if I could compete with the white students in my class who came from prestigious universities.

There was neither money nor time to do much other than study and participate at church. The first Sunday I was in Cleveland, I went to the East 100th Street Church of Christ and met Thomas O. Jackson, a businessman who owned a downtown parking lot and garage. Socializing was limited to after-church dinners with many people, including Thomas and his wife, Mattie, who was a registered nurse and a graduate of Hampton University. She did her practicum in psychiatric nursing at Tuskegee Institute. The Jacksons lived in a house behind the church. Later he sold his business in Cleveland and enrolled in Southwestern Christian College. He became a minister and served many churches across the country. He also served with me as a member of the board of trustees of Southwestern Christian College when I chaired the board. Years later he was Minister of the Tuskegee Church of Christ and died there several years ago.

I attended most church services on Sundays. When time permitted, I went to evening services and Bible Study during the week. Eventually, J. S. Winston, whom I met while I was a student at Nashville Christian Institute traveling with Bro. Keeble, became a minister and I served as his assistant. Later, the East 100th Street Church built a beautiful new building near Case Western Reserve University, and it is now known as University Church of Christ. I learned a lot about church work and human nature while working with Brother Winston. He is now deceased.

There was always a money crisis. I managed to pay fees on installments, but still owed money when the time came to take final exams. Nevertheless, I was permitted to take the exams and later paid my fees. I ranked about 20th in the class of 120; proving I could do the work.

I decided that I would work doubly hard during the summers to earn money. Unfortunately, I was unable to find employment in Cleveland during the summer after my first year, so I returned to Montgomery. The Alabama Journal needed a circulation manager for my old district, and I readily agreed to work for them that summer. Of course, I still did not have a car, so I was back on the buses.

One of the needs for the district was additional paper boys, particularly in the Tulane Court area. While searching for a paperboy in that area one day, I saw a young lady, Bernice Hill, whom I had known for some time. She lived at 560 Smythe Curve and was sitting comfortably on her front porch. I knew she was a student majoring in commerce at Alabama State College. She was also a member of the Gail Street Church of Christ, where I had preached on occasion. I went up and talked with her and asked her about a possible paperboy. She suggested several names, one of whom I employed. From that point on, Bernice and I started seeing each other, and we eventually developed a relationship. Bernice describes me as the kind of person that just grows on you. I guess she means that it takes time to get to know and like me. She really was not interested in becoming involved with a preacher, but she did.

The next summer, I remained in Cleveland, picking up and delivering clothes for a dry cleaning firm on Prospect Avenue. I was able to keep the job during the next school year. Actually, during the next summer, I worked two jobs. One was at Republic Steel in the hot metal finishing department, on the 11 p.m. to 7 a.m. shift. From there, I would go to the dry cleaners, pick up, and deliver dry cleaning in the company truck.

Despite constant money woes and the small number of African Americans, Western Reserve was an excellent university from which to receive a legal education. During my tenure there, I never experienced any unpleasantness or any form of discrimination. It proved to be the right background to prepare me to sit for the bar and for an outstanding legal career.

By my senior year, I was already studying for the Ohio and Alabama bar exams. I knew I could not take the bar review course in Alabama because of my race, but there was an Ohio bar review course being offered in Cleveland and I took it.

Becoming a Lawyer, 1954

At long last graduation day arrived. My mother and Bernice, who by that time was my fiancée, came for the commencement ceremony, and then returned to Montgomery. I remained in Cleveland to concentrate on studying. I studied day and night. This was very necessary because I was preparing myself for two bar examinations, the Ohio and Alabama. The Ohio exam was given in June and the Alabama exam in July. For the past three years, I had studied and attended law school. Now I was a law graduate, and all of the hard work would be to no avail if I did not pass the bar exams. The only way I would be able to practice law in any state would be, for the most part, to pass the bar examination of that state. While I was primarily interested in becoming a lawyer in Montgomery and carrying out my secret pledge, I was realistic enough to realize it was possible that the examiners in Alabama might discriminate against me, and regardless of what I did on the exam, they could say that I did not pass. I was taking the Ohio bar exam as a precaution.

The Alabama bar exam was scheduled for the fourth Tuesday in July. I arrived home in late June. From the moment I arrived in Montgomery, I had very little social contact with anyone; not even my fiancée Bernice. I just studied everything I could get my hands on.

Knowing enough to pass the Alabama bar exam was not the only obstacle. There were a couple of other hurdles that I had to get over before I could take the exam. Alabama required that one register as a law student by filing an application and submitting character affidavits from five lawyers who had been practicing for at least five years. I had filed the application when I enrolled in law school, but I did not know five lawyers at the time. I completed the application, admitted that I did not know five lawyers, and informed them I would submit the affidavits as soon as possible.

I was able to accomplish this task with the help of E. D. Nixon, "Mr. Civil Rights" in Montgomery, my fiancée Bernice Hill and Attorney Arthur Shores of Birmingham. With their help, I was able to get affidavits from Arthur Shores, Nesbitt Elmore, Charles Henley, Clifford Durr, W.C. Campbell, Henry Heller, and Virgil McGhee. With the exception of attorneys Shores and Henley, the other signers were with lawyers.

I took the Alabama bar exam in July 1954 and had taken the Ohio bar exam in June 1954. In August 1954, I was notified by both Ohio and Alabama that I had passed. In September 1954, I had an open house for my law office and began my practice of law in Montgomery, Alabama.

In less than six months I tried my first civil rights case, Claudette Colvin. The 15-year-old girl who did what Mrs. Rosa Parks did—refuse to give up her seat to a white person but nine months before. Subsequently, I represented Mrs. Parks, Dr. King, persons involved in the Montgomery Bus Boycott, and many more.

My Religious Background and Ministerial Work Controlled my Civil Rights Activities

During the Montgomery Bus Boycott, Bro. Bonnie Matthews, who had been dean at NCI when I was a student, came to Montgomery to hold a meeting for the Holt Street Church of Christ. It was billed to be for two weeks. He ended up holding meetings throughout the City of

Montgomery for most of the summer. At the conclusion of the meeting, he told me that the people in the Newtown community, a very depressed, ghetto area, African American community in Montgomery of low-income residents, needed a preacher. He was recommending that I preach for them. At that time I was serving as Bro. K.K. Mitchell's assistant at Holt Street. We had been classmates at NCI and I recommended him to the Elders, who employed him. I resigned that position and began working with the Newtown Church. It only had about ten members. It was located in a very poor building on a back street. But, it was a community of people who were religious, and I saw hope and prospect.

I started working with that church as I did with all the civil rights activities which you can read about in *Bus Ride to Justice*. As a result, the church began to grow and we were able to build a new building on the main street coming into the Newtown community. We later added an educational wing that housed the local Head Start Center and served as the community educational center for preschool children attending Head Start.

It was during my ministry of that church over the next almost twenty years that I was able to inspire other young men and young ladies to become gospel preachers, school principals, teachers, engineers, doctors, lawyers, church leaders, and outstanding citizens in the Montgomery community. A few of the persons that developed from that church are Charlie Chapman and Roosevelt Chapman who developed into great gospel preachers; Norris Harris, who is now minister of the Western Boulevard Church of Christ; Attorney Theron Stokes, whose grandmother, Sister Jenkins, contributed the first $100 toward the construction of the new building at Newtown. She was a great inspiration to me and helpful with the church. Theron is now the Deputy Director of the Alabama Education Association, a teacher's professional organization, and is in charge of all its legal activities. My brother-in-law Elbert Hill is a retired principal of a middle school in Montgomery. Dr. Cliff Robinson was the former chief of staff for the VA Medical Center in Tuskegee. He and his wife Cassandra Jackson grew up as members of Newtown. He is now an Elder at the Holt Street Church.

Of course, my children Deborah, Vanessa, Fred Jr. and Stanley all grew up at the Newtown and Tuskegee Churches of Christ. Fred and Stanley are partners in our law firm. Vanessa is a paralegal in the firm. Deborah is the managing director of the Tuskegee Human & Civil Rights Multicultural Center. They are all faithful members of the church.

In addition, when I became a lawyer in 1954, I was one of the few African American lawyers who were members of the Church of Christ. Probably, I was the only one who became early on, extremely involved in civil rights activities. I believe my activities in the church as a minister and elder, and a civil rights lawyer in the community, inspired many individuals, both in the Church of Christ and out of the church, to become active in civil rights activities. They realized there is space to be active in the community and civil rights, and a minister in the Lord's church.

One of the greatest rewards I have received from my two professions is to be able to see young men and ladies I have inspired go into their communities and make substantial contributions.

Blessed With Two Exceptional Christian Wives

Last but not least, the Lord blessed me with two exceptional and Christian wives. Without their help, I would not have been successful. On March 17, 1997, after 40 years of marriage, the Lord called Bernice unexpectedly. Several years later, I met and married Carol Porter of Cleveland after being introduced by Bro. Thomas O. Jackson's wife Mattie. Carol's husband Floyd had also passed a few years earlier. She and her husband were both devoted members of the Lord's Church. Carol and I were married on December 17, 2000. We enjoy a good and happy marriage. The Lord has blessed me with two wonderful Christian wives for which I am thankful. Both of them assisted me greatly in both of my professions.

Reflections

Looking back, 63 years after my admission to the bar, and after I have received many honorary degrees, various awards and honors, I never imagined when I represented those persons, that I would receive any type awards or degrees. Neither did I expect the Alabama Department of Tourism, the City of Montgomery and the City of Tuskegee to erect a historical marker in honor of me in front of the Alabama State Judicial Building on Dexter Avenue in Montgomery, and across from Lincoln Gates at the entrance to Tuskegee University's campus. I never expected Case Western Reserve University to conduct a symposium in honor of me, "Making Civil Rights Law from Rosa Parks to the Twenty-First Century," and published in a CWRU Law Review.

As a teenager in Montgomery, Alabama, I saw problems that needed to be corrected. With a lot of help, including divine help, we have been instrumental in helping to change the landscape of America, assisted in the election and re-election of the 44th President of the United States, and helping to change some conditions in the world.

My first civil rights case—representing Claudette Colvin in March 1955 and activities in connection with the Montgomery Bus Boycott, which ignited the Civil Rights Movement—were just the beginning of my 63-year career in the legal profession. That career included cases that eliminated racial discrimination in almost every aspect of American life including, but not limited to, the right to use of public transportation, vote, protect the memberships of organizations, the right to public education without discrimination, equal access to farm subsidies, health care, the right to serve on juries and many others. All of which you may read about in my autobiography, *Bus Ride to Justice.*

The history of the Civil Rights Movement must be preserved for present and future generations. Twenty years ago, we founded and have developed a history museum, the Tuskegee Human & Civil Rights Multicultural Center, which educates the public on the contributions made by the ethnic groups that have occupied and developed the land—Native Americans, Americans of European descent, and Americans of African descent. Secondly, it serves as a permanent memorial to the men in the infamous Tuskegee Syphilis Study. Thirdly, it gives a brief history of the Civil Rights Movement from slavery to the present; highlighting civil rights cases filed by residents of Macon County, Alabama, many of which were before the beginning the Montgomery Bus Boycott. We invite you to visit and to support this museum in Tuskegee, Alabama.

"Vision"

I have been asked to give my "vision" "for what I think the Restoration Movement/Stone-Campbell Movement/Churches of Christ might evolve into over the next few years." I am not an expert on the Restoration Movement Movement/Stone-Campbell Movement/ Churches of Christ. Therefore, I will not attempt to give you my "vision" of it. I will, however, share with you some facts about the New Testament Church as those facts were taught to me by various ministers of the Church of Christ located across the country. Some were ministers of the Holt Street Church of Christ, Montgomery, Alabama, William Whittaker, Sutton Johnson, Jesse T. Burson, Marshall Keeble, president of the NCI, J.W. Brent, the Bible instructor at NCI, J.S. Winston, minister of East 100th Street Church of Christ, Cleveland, Ohio, and many others. All of these ministers were African American, except J.W. Brent, who was Caucasian.

Following are some of the identifying characteristics of the Church of Christ as we find it in the New Testament and as they were taught to me:

- ITS ORIGIN: It was founded by Christ (Matthew 16:18); in Jerusalem (Luke 24:49); on the first Pentecost following the resurrection of Christ, A.D.33 (Acts 2). He bought it (Acts 20:28) and saved it (Ephesians 5:23).

- IT WAS CALLED: Churches of Christ (Romans 16:16); Church of the firstborn (Hebrews 12:23); Church of God (Acts 20:27-28); Body of Christ (Ephesians 4:12).

- LAWS OF PARDON TO UNSAVED: Hearing the Gospel (Romans 10:13-19); Believing the Gospel (Hebrews 11:6; Acts

16:31); Repenting of sins (Luke 13:35) (Acts 17:30); Confession of Jesus Christ (Luke 12:8; Romans 10:9-10; 1Peter 3:21); Baptism (Acts 2:38).

- LAWS OF PARDON TO ERRING CHRISTIAN: Repentance and prayer (Acts 8:22); Confess our sins (1 John 1:9).

- THE WORSHIP OF THE CHURCH: Must be in spirit (John 4:23); from the heart (Colossians 3:16); upon first day of week (Acts 20:1-7; Hebrew 10:25); Singing (Ephesians 5:19; Colossians 3:16; Hebrew 2:12); Prayer (Acts 2:42; 1 Timothy 2:1-2); Edifying (1 Corinthians 14:15-27); Communion (Acts 20:7; 1 Corinthians 11:20-32); Contribution (1Corinthians 16:1-2).

- WORK OF THE CHURCH:Preaching of the Gospel (1 Thessalonians 1:8; II Timothy 4:1-2); Teaching of the Gospel (1 Timothy 3:1-2; Ephesians 3:10); Visit the sick (Matthew 25: 34-40); Feed the hungry (Acts 6:1-5; James 2:15); Caring for the fatherless and widows (James 1:27).

Now I have shared with you some facts about the New Testament Church as I was taught. The Church of Christ's doctrines and beliefs are based on the New Testament. The church belongs to Christ, and Christ's word has not changed since it was recorded by inspired men of God who wrote them as directed by the Holy Spirit. In Acts 2, we read what it took to become Christians on the first Pentecost following the resurrection of Christ; it takes the same today to become a member of the church.

My "vision" for the church is that the church would remain and continue to be the church established by Christ speaking where the Bible speaks; and being silent where the Bible is silent.

Back in the Day
by Paul Watson

I was born on April 8, 1939, in St. Joseph Hospital in Houston, Texas, the first child of Frank and Alice Watson. My first religious experience came in that same hospital some three years later, when my dad took me there to see my new-born baby sister. As we got into the elevator, two "sisters" in full religious habit got on behind us. As the elevator doors closed, I buried my face in my father's pants leg, knowing death was imminent. I first experienced the joy of salvation when the elevator stopped, the doors opened, and we were allowed to escape.

Otherwise, I was a "child of the church"—the Church of Christ. My mother had been immersed as a teenager in a congregation in Branson, MO. My father, a lapsed Catholic when he and mother married, was baptized about six months before I was at the Lawndale Church of Christ in Houston, Texas. Lawndale was a "church plant" of the old Central congregation in Houston where my parents originally worshipped. Years before I was baptized, I gave my first "sermon"—actually a recitation of the Beatitudes from memory—at the age of five. Lawndale continued to nurture me until I left for ACC and Abilene in 1957. I remember in particular Brother Max T. Neel, who baptized me and gave me my first "preachin' Bible"—a small, flexible copy of the "New Testament with Psalms" that would fit into the breast pocket of a suit coat. And I remember Brother Herman Page, who would take a half-dozen of us rowdy junior high boys into the church balcony every Sunday morning for Bible class—what a saint he was to put up with us.

Looking back, Lawndale was "right" on all the "issues" of the day—knew what the shibboleths were and carefully avoided them. But, more importantly, Lawndale was a loving, receptive congregation that showed concern both for members and for the community around us. I, along with so many others, was a recipient of that nurturing love.

As I say, I went to Abilene in the fall of 1957 and enjoyed every moment of my four years there. I majored in Greek, minored in Bible, English, and history. So many of the professors there had a shaping influence on my life, none perhaps more so than Dr. J. W. Roberts. He taught me Greek and Bible in the classroom, but he also taught me outside of class. On Boy Scout camping trips (where I served as Dr. Roberts' assistant Scout Master), after the scouts went to their tents at night, he and I would sit around the campfire and talk about Christianity, Christian scholarship, and life in general. And I recall Dr. Paul Southern, chairman of the Bible Department, talking with us in Greek class about pastoral counseling from time to time. I recall once asking Dr. Southern how he kept from getting depressed himself, listening to other people's problems all the time. "Oh, I just lock the problems in my office when I go home every afternoon so I can enjoy my family." At the time, I thought that about as cruel and indifferent a comment as I had ever heard from a preacher. Years later, with experience, I came to appreciate its wisdom. Other professors whom I considered mentors include Dr. Lemoine Lewis in Bible, Dr. James Culp in English and Dr. Ed Brown in speech and debate. I was privileged to be in the audience the night Dr. Carl Spain gave his now-famous sermon on race relations in the church and the college, and I remain deeply affected both by what he said and how he said it.

Like most "preacher-boys," I preached for one of the small, rural congregations near Abilene—the Lindsay Chapel Church of Christ. The church building sat on the edge of a cotton field not far from the town of Lueders, Texas. That small group of saints will surely have an abundance of stars in their crowns, listening patiently and encouragingly as they did to so many sermons over so many years by so many "preacher-boys" like me. I learned so much more from them than they ever learned from me, I'm sure. Brother Howell (pronounced "Hal") Cobb was perhaps the best adult Bible class teacher I've have ever heard. And I observed one older member help his wife die from cancer, lovingly caring for her at their home for almost a year until she passed away, then within six months himself dying, having finished his work on this earth.

After my sophomore year at ACC I married my high school sweetheart, Mary Ann Henderson. We would eventually have four children—Mark, Susan, Beth, and Meg—of whom I remain quite proud. Ann and I were married some twenty-four years until she died in an automobile accident not long after we had moved to Durham, North Carolina, to work with the Cole Mill Road congregation there. But I'm getting ahead of myself.

In the spring of my senior year at Abilene, a life-changing event for me occurred when Dr. Jack Scott—a fellow panelist today—visited Abilene to recruit students to come to Yale for their graduate education and to work with the Whitney Avenue congregation in New Haven. Jack "sold" me, and I redirected my steps from Harvard to Yale Divinity School. My first year there was Jack's last year and, when Jack left for California, I took his place as pulpit minister for the church, serving in this capacity for the next three years as I completed my B.D. (now, M.Div.). I then entered Yale's Ph.D. program. Having come to appreciate the beauty and the value of the Old Testament, I concentrated in Old Testament studies and was fortunate enough to be taught and mentored by Dr. Brevard Childs, arguably the most influential Old Testament scholar of his generation. What may not be as well known is that Professor Childs was also a dedicated churchman who saw his academic work as being done in the service of the Church. And when it was his turn to preach in chapel, you had to be early to get a seat.

Having finished my coursework, but not my dissertation, in 1968 I moved from New Haven CT to Due West, South Carolina, to begin my teaching career at Erskine College, a small private college supported by the Associate Reformed Presbyterian Church. My family and I attended the Clemson Church of Christ, where I also preached from time to time. After four years in Due West, Jack Scott came calling again, this time to join a team planning an innovative general education curriculum for the new Pepperdine campus being built on the hillsides of Malibu. Again, while in California, I preached for the Woodland Hills Church of Christ while helping to develop the new curriculum.

However, my tenure at Pepperdine was brief. After only a year in L.A., we moved back to South Carolina and Erskine, where I taught in the Bible department and subsequently served as Dean of Students. From 1979 to 1983, I served as professor of Biblical studies in the Institute for Christian Studies (now Austin Graduate School of Theology) in Austin, Texas. I also preached for several churches in the Austin area from time to time, most notably the Church of Christ in Lockhart, Texas.

You are getting the picture, I'm sure: one foot behind the lectern, one foot in the pulpit. Although I enjoyed both lectern and pulpit, I decided that to be most effective, I needed to choose one or the other. So, in 1983, when a vacancy in the Cole Mill Road congregation in Durham, North Carolina came open, I applied for, and was hired for, the position. This meant leaving behind a son already in college and a daughter ready to start college there in Texas, as well as leaving behind my parents, my only sibling (my sister, Patricia), and all my good colleagues and friends at ICS. Nevertheless, it seemed clear to me that this was a move God was calling me to make. It turned out to be a good move, a right move. For the next twenty-four years, I served as senior minister for the congregation and, for twenty-two years, as an elder.

Cole Mill Road is somewhat unique in that it has been, and still is, a "town-and-gown" church in which both "town" and "gown" are mutually supportive, not antagonistic. CMR serves as the "campus church" both for Duke University (Durham) and the University of North Carolina (Chapel Hill), as well as attracting students from Durham Tech, Meredith College (Raleigh), and other nearby schools. The church has consistently seen one large part of its particular mission to support the spiritual growth of such students while they are here in school, as well as to equip them to become church leaders as they move on to new locations and vocations.

Another large part of CMR's mission has been to support me in my "scholarly" contributions to the church at large. Thus the congregation not only allowed but encouraged me to write articles and to speak on lectureships, sermon seminars, and other public forums. They also helped send me and my wife Kay (see below) on some five mission trips to St. Petersburg, Russia, to work with the Institute for Theology and Christian Ministry and the Neva congregation there. CMR saw such efforts as another way of ministering to the church at large. In turn, I tried never to abuse their trust but to fulfill faithfully all of my "regular" ministerial duties—visitation of the sick, pastoral counseling, conducting weddings and funerals, teaching, and of course preaching.

In addition to two major building projects on the church campus, there have been three significant events over the course of my ministry at Cole Mill Road. The first of these events was the death of my first wife, Ann, in an automobile accident and my subsequent remarriage to Virginia Kay Roberts, herself a widow who had lost her husband Jim a few months after Ann died. Kay and I met in the foyer of our church building after a morning worship service, when a deacon's wife whose two daughters had been Kay's piano students called out in a voice that carried across the hall, "You'll have to meet our preacher; he lost his wife too." For perhaps the only time in my ministerial career, I was speechless. Kay found the words, "Are you doing okay?" and I finally responded, "I guess so; how about you?" Three years later, we were married in the family room of her mother's home. This November, the Lord willing, Kay and I will celebrate our twenty-eighth wedding anniversary. As hard as it was, living through the grief of loss and the ache of recovery tempered me in ways that must be experienced to be understood. And finding love again, and meeting the challenge of "blending" two existing families, has also had a profound shaping effect on me, and, I think, on my ministry.

The second significant event was the discovery that one of our elders was a pedophile who had been abusing children of the congregation over a period of some years. As one would imagine, it was a startling, devastating discovery that first came to light at midnight on a Saturday night when a member called to inform me what had happened to his daughter. Thus began a long, hard process, led by the elders, of discovery and of interaction with the offending elder, with the local authorities, and with our members, some of whom would not believe what had transpired, some of whom wanted to lynch the offender on the spot. It took weeks and even months of close cooperation among the elders and frequent interactions with the congregation to accept the reality of what had happened; to respond to that reality according to scriptural principles and with much prayer; and, eventually, to move on.

The third major event—actually, a series of events—has to do with the elder-led decision by the congregation to become gender-inclusive in worship leadership (except for preaching) and in teaching adult Bible classes. The elders studied this issue on three separate occasions over a period of years until we reached the conclusion that (a) such gender-inclusion was in keeping with the teachings and examples of Scripture, and (b) the time had come for our particular congregation to adopt such a practice. The elders presented our findings to the congregation in a series of ten Sunday morning joint adult Bible classes [which are available on request to the church office], followed on Sunday evenings by a small group, elder-led discussions of the morning presentations. As you can imagine, not all members concurred with the decision, and about forty members left us to start a new congregation.

Three things in that process stand out for me: First, the elders did not "yield to the demands" of "uppity women." We had no "uppity women" demanding their "rights," but rather a number of gifted women who wanted to share their gifts with the congregation, if the elders and the congregation so willed. Second, we did not, and do not, place "quotas" on participation. On a given Sunday morning, we might have seven or eight women serving in various capacities; on another Sunday, there might be two or three. Third, we did not, and do not, put pressure on any woman to participate. We recognize that some are gifted for reading Scripture, leading singing, etc., while some are not —just like the men of the congregation. (As a footnote, this past June the elders announced that they had come to the further decision that women could preach from the pulpit; and two women have done so in the past ten months.)

After serving the congregation for some twenty-four years, I retired to "preacher/elder emeritus" status in 2007 but have remained, with Kay, an active participant in the congregation. And I have "reverted" to my other vocational love, that of teaching. For some fourteen years now I have served, first part-time, now full-time, as professor of Bible and Christian ministry for Amridge University in Montgomery, Alabama. Since Amridge is now a completely "on-line" institution, I teach from home with only occasional trips to the campus. This summer, I am teaching courses in the Psalms and in homiletics, and, as always, am delighted to work with students—many of whom are older, second-career students. I also serve from time to time as a mentor to student-members at Cole Mill Road who are enrolled in Duke Divinity School and who do an internship year with the congregation. It is always gratifying to work with such students, whether older or younger, who want to receive the training that will equip them for greater service in the Kingdom.

The Larger Picture

From my viewpoint, over the past fifty years or so, three "trends" have developed in churches of Christ. The first has been the increased emphasis on a trained ministry—academically trained professors with Ph.D. degrees from prestigious institutions initially; pastorally trained ministers with M.Div. and D. Min. degrees more recently. With such training has come a move away from intellectual rigidity and doctrinal inflexibility—"legalism," in other words—toward a better understand, and deeper appreciation, of Scripture. We have come to see that Christianity and the New Testament do not begin with Acts 2 and Pentecost but with Jesus and the four Gospels. Similarly, the Old Testament—quoted so often by Jesus and Paul—is still Scripture and continues to speak great truths to our minds and hearts.

A second development has been the move toward a more "enthusiastic" style of worship. I can remember my father, on a family vacation trip from Texas to the Northeast, commenting that, "any Church of Christ you visit on a Sunday morning will have exactly the same worship"—and he meant that as compliment and reassurance. Such, of course, is not the case today. Informality in worship forms and even in the attire of worshippers has become the order of the day. "Praise Teams" are common, albeit in various forms (but no "Lament Teams," at least as far as I am aware). Even—shudder!—instrumental music, at least in some services; for it is not uncommon for a large congregation with multiple services to have a "traditional" liturgy at the 11:00 service but a more "progressive" liturgy at the 9:00 service. Furthermore, services that coincide with the Christian Year—Advent, Lent, Easter, Pentecost—are becoming increasingly common. This is quite different from my "growing-up" years when "Christmas" was only a "family holiday," and *every* Sunday was "Easter" Sunday.

One exception to these changes in worship has been the general retention of our weekly observance of the Lord's Supper, a practice that is often noted approvingly by leaders in other communions. For example, Dr. Stanley Hauerwas (a classmate from my days at Yale) liked to say that he had no hope of ever persuading his Methodist students to offer communion every Sunday; but he did hope to make them feel guilty every Sunday they did *not* celebrate the Eucharist.

The third shift that I have noted—one that is ongoing—is the inclusion of women in worship roles, in adult Bible teaching, and in church leadership positions (i.e., as deacons and as children's ministers). This shift has proved to be hard to make, or hard not to make—hard intellectually, harder still emotionally and practically. The difficulty undoubtedly has to do with (a) how we read Scripture, and (b) how we read gender-relations in our society. For example, one minister related a conversation that he had had with a male leader in his congregation who vociferously opposed any change. "Why," the minister asked, "are you so opposed even to considering such a change?" "Because," the man replied, "in every other aspect of my life, my wife calls the shots: where we live, how we spend our money, where we go on vacation. She's the boss, everywhere—except in church. Then it's my turn."

And in the Future?

I have no crystal ball, only some (partially) educated guesses as to what the future might hold for churches of Christ. As suggested by the previous paragraph, I do not see the "women's roles" issue going "gentle into that good night." There are simply too many women (and men), both younger and older, who want to see more female participation and leadership in our churches. And many of these women (and men) are in a position, as professors in the Bible departments of our Christian colleges and as church leaders, to lead and facilitate such a change. How quickly this development will come, and what it will do to relationships between churches that "do" include women and churches that "don't," I have no idea.

One salutary development that I sense is the continued desire by our younger brothers and sisters both to get advanced degrees in theology and ministry and to use that advanced training, if possible, in and for churches within the Stone-Campbell tradition. I know that Cole Mill Road is not your typical Stone-Campbell congregation. Nevertheless, we have a young man, trained at Duke but nurtured by CMR, who will begin his ministry with a congregation in northeast Texas in July. And we have a young woman, similarly trained and nurtured, who will become a faculty member in the Bible department at ACU this September. Moreover, we have at least three men and two women in various stages of their academic training in theology, plus at least one more couple coming this fall. And we have two students—one male, one female—who will receive their joint M.Div. / M.D. degrees this spring. An even better gauge to this burgeoning interest in theological education and discussion is this very Christian Scholars Conference, with its emphasis on younger scholars presenting papers and serving on panels. The outstanding question in this regard, I think, is whether or not these young theologians will be able to find places of service in Stone-Campbell churches that will not simply accept them but will value, and utilize, their training.[1]

If I have a major concern for the future, it is about postmodernism in general and its potential influence on our churches and on these young leaders-to-be in particular. To distance ourselves from a sterile rationalism is one thing; to embrace emotion-driven individualism would be quite another. I hope we will not rush to that end of the see-saw. Instead, I hope that we will combine mind, heart, and will in new and

---

[1] This is the very topic that a panel discussion will address at this conference: "Athens and Jerusalem: the Intersection of Academia and Ministry in Churches of Christ."

creative ways that will inspire us to use every God-given gift to bring in the Kingdom and give Him the glory.

A Recall of Personalities, Opportunities, and Involvements by Andrew J. Hairston

INTRODUCTION

It is my honored privilege to have been invited by Gayle Crowe to be one of several ministers to present at the June 2017 Christian Scholars Conference. The challenge is great and far-reaching. To put forward individuals and events that have led us to become the church leaders that God has blessed us to be is no small task. This challenge spreads across many years and experiences – many of which are no longer aspects of our memories.

A foremost aim of my life has always been to be God's man – with my family, in pursuits, and in carrying out God's will as his minister. Once I understood what it really meant to accept Jesus as Lord, at an early age, that basic choice has sustained me in life as a learner under God.

We have an eternal fight with an able enemy. Yet, though the weapons of our warfare are not carnal, "they are mighty through God" who assures us of the victory to the extent of giving Christ the victory through the enemy's ultimate weapon, the cross.

Among the challenges met by us who are committed to pushing forward for God are the internal challenges of commitment to Christ, self-denials, and those major built-in stubborn structural feature of gender, racial discriminations, cultural issues, economic biases and other built and naturalized biases which we have normalized to deepen such sins in our lives.

My Undergirding Philosophy of Faith

Regarding and undergirding "what has made me the minister I am" lies a fundamental faith foundation of my relationship with God, Christ, Church, and self. Beneath and supporting me is a deep fundamental acceptance of Christ and His Church; this relationship exists as a clearinghouse connecting the church and my life. Such is the philosophy and the process for my thinking and action through which my life is processed for approval and sanctioned preceding my conduct. As a result, I seek not only to bring Christ and His gospel to believers; I struggle with bringing myself as an example of the living message.

Accordingly, undergirding my life and ministry is a committed determination to know God and his power as referenced by Paul in Philippians and to seize the opportunity to have free range in my life to do His will.

MEMOIRS

By way of background, I was born July 8, 1932, the thirteenth of fifteen children born to James and Laura Hairston in Clemmons, N.C. At six years old, I watched my father die and to this day clearly recall actions attending his demise—actions which included my sleeping in the room with his body on the nights before the funeral.

Even though I was aware that my family was poor and without resources, I easily remember a deep and aggravating concern that my daddy died in an all but penniless state— leaving my mother without references or resources and a half dozen children still living at home. I was so impressed with the state of poverty in which my mother had been left that I stole away from the family gathered at the fireplace to check daddy's money pocketbook to find that he had only one crumpled-up dollar bill to his name. That discovery so devastated me that my mind did not register any memory of subsequent actions or thoughts.

It was at an early age in Clemmons that I walked through the woods with my mother on Sunday mornings to attend worship services held at a boy's boarding school. I vividly recall the schoolmaster and minister of the Church of Christ that met in the school which evangelized residents in Clemmons and surrounding areas. My mother's sister was a church member. She taught and converted my mother. I have no recall of my father ever attending church.

Influential Personalities and Events Affecting My Life

Regarding impacts on me as a Christian and gospel minister, it was Christ, his disciples, and the early church leaders who are my early heroes. Jesus Christ is the centerpiece of my life because He placed God's will above His own by choosing Calvary when all was at stake. For me, Christ was and is the example of control in making the right and best choice, which is by far a critical support of life. Even in the overwhelming depth of sin, loneliness, and abandonment, Christ demonstrated the clear ability to elect to follow the right and difficult path to complete His divine assignment. When all went wrong, Jesus lived out the right. His commitment to God allowed Him to find and pursue the right in the midst of sin. He well described His ability in the words, "I must always do the will of Him that sent me" (John 4:34). He is, for me, the unforgettable example of determined obedience in lowly and extremely challenging times.

My mother was the example of a relationship with God, Christ, conditions, the church, and committed determination. Such factors are deeply rooted in my life and push me toward its righteous destiny. Because of her, my life is inseparably bound to Christ and His Church. Her exemplary faith and devotion have marked and anchored my life in Christ. To copy Jesus' words in response to Pilate, "to this end was I born and for this cause came I into the world, that I should bear witness to the truth" (John 18:37). It is with this quality of determination that I, like Jesus, seek to copy his commitment who while asking for relief from Calvary's death no less than three times, demonstrated his power of faith to surrender to Calvary as he understood God willed.

Jeanne, my wife of 61 years, deserves high and strong recognition. She consistently contributed without limitation as she put God's ways ahead of our way by always yielding to His course of action when it conflicted with hers.

Gospel preachers have been great sources for my development. Without respect or restriction as to our being children or adult, ministers related to us and included us in the life of the church. Rather than not include us as youth, we were welcomed. Throughout my life in Christ, it has been my blessing to be received and encouraged by church leaders and the church.

Southwestern Christian College and Gus Farmer, my Bible and Greek instructor, were timely, strong, and unforgettable jolts to my life. Gus was a great blessing to my life. Beyond being my teacher, we became great friends, a friendship that lasted until his death. He was my mentor and came into my life at a good time. He was an exceptional model for me, becoming the door that expanded my approach to the Bible and its uses in my journey for God among mortals. Gus and his approach to the issues of God, Christ, Church, and believers exposed me to a more God-involved perception that proved to be a blessing which, without Gus, I may not have ever known.

It was my blessing to meet Keeble, who inspired thousands. I once heard him say that he had baptized no less than 40,000 souls. He established the Simpson Street Church of Christ in a four-weekend Tent Gospel Meeting in 1931 which reaped 166 baptisms. Keeble was a Black Icon evangelist who hardly completed grade school.

Keeble impacted my life for good and provided me with a strong positive example. He amazed me with his ability to relate to all groups. From him, I learned gratitude and the importance of all people. Keeble was a natural. People flocked to hear him. He inspired me to work to be my best and to scale the highest heights. He lived out the Pauline statement, "I have learned, in whatever state I am, therewith to be content" (Philippians 4:11).

I was positively challenged by Reuel Lemmons, who possessed an extensive knowledge of the Bible. With his connected knowledge of the Bible, he had an enviable knowledge and grasp of the scripture. Reuel had an impressive grasp of the "word." His knowledge and controlling possession of the Bible, the word, secured the listener's attention. His exemplary possession and proclamation of the scriptures showed him to be a man of the "book." His example was impressive and inspired me to want to "know" the Bible as he did. He encouraged me to believe that I "must" know and apply the scriptures as an indispensable divine resource and tool.

Effects of Spiritual and Academic Studies

The Simpson Street Opportunity

My biblical and theological training beyond membership in the church has been a true blessing to me. This level of education helped me to put into action my biblical knowledge beyond just trying to develop a broader foundation. It helped me to prepare for and recognize the world beyond the protected life of the disciplined church and the people to whom God is calling us to minister. There always seemed to have been support from God supplying a direction or discipline to which I was drawn and which related to the ministry of the God's word and church, according to the time and place of my involvement.

When I was but 29 years old in 1961, Alonzo Rose, a prior minister of the Simpson Street Church of Christ in Atlanta, Georgia, recommended me to the church's leadership to fill the pulpit which had been vacant for two years following the resignation of Arthur Perkins. This opportunity followed my receipt of my Bachelor of Divinity and nearing the completion of my Masters of Theology at Brite School of Divinity in Fort Worth, Texas. I believed that God was guiding me and revealing that Atlanta afforded Him and me the opportunity to get involved in a significant way for His church and the Civil Rights Movement. I discussed with Simpson Street's leadership the idea of continuing my education and of becoming involved in the movement if I moved to Atlanta. The church sanctioned the plan.

Being chosen to serve a church founded by Keeble whose image was not one of pro-civil rights was, to say the least, a sensitive matter. My involvement in Civil Rights was initiated by my meeting Fred Bennett, a Baptist minister, who was the movement's secretary to Dr. Martin Luther King, Jr. of the Southern Christian Leadership Conference. I saw this as an introduction to the movement as permitted by God to open a new avenue of services to me. I believed it was an important step toward bringing divine judgment to an oppressed people with whom I identified in and beyond the church.

I soon became an active member of the movement's subunit, Operation Breadbasket, where I met with other ministers and Civil Rights workers on a regular and continuing basis.

Joining and becoming active in the Civil Rights Movement exposed me to many of the significant personalities of the area across the face of humanity who focused on addressing the problems of our citizens without discrimination and to the exclusion of church or religious differences. To say the least, this afforded me a frontal exposure to further introduce Christ and His church to society and to become a known productive part of the community. Because there were no ministers of the Churches of Christ that I knew other than Attorney Fred Gray involved in the Civil Rights organizations, my presence brought welcomed and unbelievable attention to my involvement and to our church. This and other involvements moved our church to the forefront of community recognition and allowed us to advertise as "A Church with a Community Focus." Our church was even more welcomed for its food, clothing, rental assistance, and Substance Abuse programs. Participating in positive marches, sharing in rallies for better jobs and employment and being involved in the community programs regarding Missing and Murdered Children exposed our church to unlimited opportunities to address and to minister to victims of real needs.

It was in this period that I entered and graduated from Law School for the express purpose of giving the Civil Rights Movement and our members capable representation before the courts and to be one of the founders and incorporators of Concerned Black Clergy ministers of Metropolitan Atlanta, an organization of ministers dedicated to addressing issues of concern for our communities and their environs.

Academic Opportunities

Upon coming to Atlanta, I enrolled in Atlanta University for the Master Degree in Sociology. This merger of Sociology and Theology proved beneficial to my better understanding of working with and through people. It enhanced my understanding and prepared me to serve in and support the founding and operation of the Liberian Mission in Monrovia, Liberia in 1969, a work that yet stands, 45 years later, as an exemplary and productive effort of a faith jointly founded by Dr. Roosevelt Wells of New York and me.

Still further, my captioned opportunities of learning have been productive at home and beyond in the development of leadership classes, building church education programs, and developing ministries. We produced helpful materials and developed other needed, productive classes, Strategic Plans, property acquisition, developing a strong Strategic Plan for the church and other productive ideas. This inspired ministers to use their talents and resources to serve the Lord of Life and His creation through substance abuse programs, parental/child classes, and other resources that spoke to human needs. Simpson Street became recognized as a viable "church" in a community in decline.

Advantages of Legal Education

The legal path offered outlets of spiritual service to me that I never envisioned. I began as a solo practicing attorney followed by becoming as an Assistant Fulton County Prosecutor, then moved up to Atlanta's second City Solicitor ever, and finally retired as Atlanta City Traffic Judge. At each level, I was able to impress and to influence more souls for Christ and to educate our congregation in legal dealings that soon elevated its position in the community. The community took pride in having a minister who was also available as a lawyer.

At all levels of my educational development and involvement in the community, I was also viewed as a minister living out the ministry of involvement through the church in the Atlanta Community and beyond. My advances in law, theology, military and otherwise brought a strong positive and influential pastoral image of Christ to His Church, to our membership and the world in which it, the church, was in control and functionally active, as a vibrant part of the community that gave me involvement in the issue of Missing and Murdered Children, the incorporation of the church and exposure of our believers in more practical ways which resulted in the church's self-appreciation and its Outreach Ministry. Without doubt, Simpson Street is recognized as a church redemptively involved in the local community and beyond. It appears that Simpson Street is Atlanta's only church to which the City has awarded its minister a Historical Marker highlighting the minister and his life.

In my broadening educational community and civil rights involvement, my understanding of ministry as compared to preaching took on new and inclusive involvements. I have come to understand better and to search for ways to relate with improved focus on those to whom I seek to minister. The chaplaincy, sociology, law, and real estate focused me more on people to whom I sought to bring the message in new forms. This gave an improved focus to my ministry.

Military Chaplaincy

Out of my patriotism, love for my country, and in support of those who serve in the defense of our country, I chose to volunteer my services to our country in the Chaplaincy Branch of the U.S. Army Reserve. This contributed significantly to my involvement and development. It afforded me acquaintance, exposure, and learning opportunity in meeting, sharing, and serving mankind in a different model of ministry. I was blessed much and became a more relaxed godly servant of God in His world of human creation. Rising from First Lieutenant through the ranks to the level of Unit Supervisory Chaplain and beyond, allowed me the experience of supervision, setting and designing programs and serving directly under the Commanding General of military units. This became a two-way learning and benefit-impacting experience. It was a meaningful opportunity to advance the gospel message to my troops and to use the organizational and military structural knowledge to the ongoing development of my general ministry. It was also an impacting opportunity to serve and to grow when my Reserve Unit was called to Active Duty during the times of Desert Shield and Desert Storm. It was a challenge to engage the men and women in counseling who were answering the call.

Visions

Present issues and concerns at work in our brotherhood force us to see a vision distinctively different from what the vision might have been at the founding of the church.

The church is God's instrument of holistic redemption of humanity, and we are charged with implementing His will through His church. Yet and though God's will for His church is perfect man, through the absence of concentrated attention on the will of God, we have often faltered on the mission. Failure to follow through on God's will allows evil to enter and to control.

Just as Adam and Eve and others who followed them allowed SIN to distract and to derail them, a similar process appears to be at work in God's church today. The call of God is deep and far-reaching. Such represents our past and impacts our future. History has shown that we appear to be too earth connected to fully pursue God's heaven-bound goals.

Though knowing and loving truth, we have not pursued it as to its time and of deliverance. The sins of division, preference, disorganization, paternalism, ethnicity, gender bias, and racism have claimed the victory for ages, even since before Joel's prophecy of promised salvation and unity.

Our seeming unwillingness to work against our wills taking priority over God's will and openly disallowing the efforts of internal decline and the shifts of worship to float the church toward ideas that take us away from the Lord, questions about our destiny is hardly questionable and are destined to adversely affect who we are and who and what we hope to be.

Signs are that we are giving place to concerns that make us more comfortable in the larger religious world. The present church appears to be without pointed distinctive pleas for biblical dexterity, scriptural relevance, and identity while retaining its search for truth. Yet, such phenomena may have caused the church to function or operate beneath a seeming siege of growing in distinction, change for accommodation, materialism, entertainment and other low profile changes imparting factors that are subject to affect change to the church's image. Such is destined to weaken God's plan and bears the promise of a negative reward.

It is my hope that the church will not perish from the earth. However, the question of the church's future appearance and markings are important issues. That "future church" will bear the weight of defining and representing God regardless of the brightness or dimness of its light.

In this writing I have sought to describe and to reference my involvement with persons, events and circumstances associated with and/or contributed to my being "the person/minister of recognition and respect that I am," while striving to live life as best as I could for God and others as is evidenced by the life of Christ.

Please receive and express my deep appreciation to those at the Christian Scholars' Conference for this humbling opportunity to serve the cause of our Maker.

Let Me Tell You a Story
by Robert Randolph

I am a cradle Campbellite. I have no qualms about the designation. To deny history is foolish, to willfully ignore history in the service of a theological position, e.g., to hold that we leap over history in order to present ourselves as first century Christians, is a scandal.

The significance of the declaration is because the church was/is important to my family. Everything revolved around the church when I came into this world. California was a land of endless possibilities and temptations. The church served the young couples who had gravitated west during the Great Depression. The church was the antidote to Woody Guthrie's judgment:

> *Oh, if you ain't got the do re mi folks,*
> *...*
> *Why you better go back to beautiful Texas*
> *Oklahoma, Kansas, Georgia, Tennessee.*
> *California is a garden of Eden, a paradise*
> *To live in or see;*
> *But believe it or not, you won't find it so hot*
> *If you ain't got the do re me.*[1]

The congregation I was born into was started in July 1940. My parents had both been born in Texas, five years apart, but theirs was a marriage that united divergent strands of our Church of Christ history. Dad's parents were dry land farmers, and Dad was born in Trent, Texas. He

---

[1] *Do Re Me*, by Woody Guthrie.

grew up in Thalia, Texas in Foard County, near Vernon and Wilbarger County. In my early years, I believed Thalia to be the capital of Texas. Thalia produced at least two Church of Christ preachers of some note. Wright Randolph, my uncle, and John Banister who ministered in Dallas for nearly fifty years.

Uncle Wright and Banister personified two distinct strands of our version of the Restoration Movement. Wright was self-educated, Banister studied at Harding College and taught school for a few years while preaching in Thalia. Wright followed Route 66 to California; Banister stayed close to home and ended up at the largest Church of Christ in Dallas and produced a book of sermons in the Great Preachers of Today series. He preached on television for nearly 40 years in the Dallas-Fort Worth area.

Wright's congregations were less noteworthy, and he became a voice of the non-institutional Churches of Christ as that division became more vocal in the 1950s and 1960s. Not one to write books, Wright did write articles in the papers that flourished in the mid-20th century. He was described by one peer as one "We might not have always agreed with him, but we never…doubted his convictions." I once met a man who had been "converted" by Wright. "He argued me into the Church of Christ," said this former Baptist.

My mother was born near Sherman, Texas, as my grandfather, E.W. McMillan began his career as a preacher in the Churches of Christ. Widowed in 1921, Grandfather had been strongly influenced by Elizabeth Baxter's belief in the importance of education. The role of the Baxter family in the history of higher education in Churches of Christ is well known. Grandfather began his education at Gunter Bible School, took degrees from Austin College and Baylor and was ABD from Southwestern Baptist Seminary in Fort Worth.

Mother completed high school in Abilene while her father was preaching for the College Church of Christ and head of the Bible Department at ACC. She went on to take degrees from David Lipscomb College and George Pepperdine College in Los Angeles. It was in L.A. that my parents met and they were married in the Vermont Avenue Church of Christ shortly after she graduated in 1939. I was born a year later.

I retell his history so that the strands of our movement's history may be sensed if not understood. "Buy the truth and sell it not," was Wright's favorite text. Bro. Mc preached about the power of the gospel as likened to the mighty Mississippi River, overwhelming everything in its path. Long on rhetorical flourish, he was short on arguing, and it is no surprise that the greatest early influence on my religious education was my Grandfather.

The second influence was what I think of as context. I might have been born into the structured southern environment of Nashville or the frontier environment of Abilene, but I grew up in the California of the Campbellite diaspora. The canvas was already painted with more than 300 years of Spanish presence, but there was a sense we were doing something new. I certainly felt that going to church. Each Sunday, we gathered for worship and to celebrate the accomplishments of our immigrant community. When the war ended, the signs of success were to be seen in new cars and new homes. We were a chosen people, and our success confirmed that we were doing something right.

My family tried to break out of the pattern by moving back to Tennessee, where Grandfather was confident there was an opportunity for my father. We moved in early winter of 1945 after my father took leave from his position in the Post Office. The experiment lasted less than a year but embedded in my mind certain markers that would shape my self-understanding.

On the way east in New Mexico, our car overturned on an icy road. That no one was injured was a small miracle. That our family was taken in by a Mexican family while we sought to repair the car so we could continue on our journey was life-altering. Obviously poor by our standards, these folks took us in, kept us warm and comforted us while the necessary issues were dealt with. They were Catholic; the experience of being the stranger has not been forgotten.

We continued to Memphis, but by the summer, my father and I were on our way back to California. We had been living in the minister's home next to the Union Avenue Church of Christ. Union Avenue was a social force in Memphis, unlike any congregation we had ever experienced. Bro. Mc was known in the city as an opinion shaper. It was a far cry from our rented quarters occupied by the church in Southern

California. There were no surprises when you came to church in Memphis. There was the power of wealth, and the smell of a closed church opened on Sunday morning. And there was the issue of race.

My family was not prepared for the realities of racial protocols and traditions. Obviously, the story was more complicated than I remember, but our return to California was occasioned by a business meeting in which the judgment of the church was that rats were not an issue so long as they remained in the black sexton's house at the rear of the church. My father was not willing to raise his children in such a world.

He returned to his civil service job with its protections, and we found a small house on the edge of the growing San Fernando Valley. We were close enough to continue to drive to Burbank despite the fact that there was soon another congregation of the Church of Christ within a few miles of our house. Batsell Barrett Baxter was our preacher in Burbank; Frank Pack followed him in the pulpit. My father once noted that when Hoyt Houchen preached at the Van Nuys congregation, you could hear him on our front porch. Implicit was the comparison with Burbank where shouting was not the order of the day.

As we resettled in California, E.W. McMillan began to travel to Japan to lay the foundation for mission efforts as the war ended. He continued to do so as he raised money for Ibaraki Christian College. He often stayed with our family on layovers, and sometimes he took me to meetings raising money for the efforts in Japan.

In addition to Japan, he also began to work with the new college in Terrell, Texas, called Southwestern Christian College. Eventually, as President, he moved to the campus, and for summers, my siblings and I would spend time on the campus of the fledgling college begun to offer the opportunity for higher education to Negroes.

Each summer, I would walk across the railroad tracks into a black world. My playmates were boys my own age, and I learned early what it meant to be a minority. I experienced segregation in real time when we went to the movies downtown and I had to sit separated from my friends. Later, going to church on campus my friend Clarence Carpenter and I staged a walk-out because the minister had said that only members of the Church of Christ would be in heaven. That gesture ended our opportunity to go to church together.

Terrell was not my first experience with being the outsider. When my mother began teaching, it was easier for me to attend school where she taught, and so I went with her to a predominately Hispanic school. I do not remember any discomfort and enjoyed learning to communicate in Spanish on the playground. There I also learned the social structure of the school. The older girls called the shots and you did not resist their leadership. I was the only Anglo boy in the school, and apparently my social skills needed some sharpening. I watched, listened, and learned. Again, the experiment was short-lived, and soon I was back in an Anglo school, but I left with a lifetime of experiences to reflect upon.

The shaping influence of my Grandfather and the California context were mediated by the church. Growing up in the congregation meant the steady exposure to people who cycled through. Pilots in the emerging airline industry came and went. We all mourned the death of a former member in a Wyoming plane crash in 1955. There were also those in the entertainment industry, radio, movies, the early days of television. I have never attended worship services when the vocal quality of those who welcomed us to worship matched those who led worship at the Burbank congregation. Taking Sunday morning seriously was etched on my psyche by those making announcements and calling us to worship.

Then there was the reality that we were in California. On Saturdays, it was not uncommon for groups to gather at the beach coming to worship sunburned on Sunday. The beach culture was part of our world.

When it came time to go to college, I was unprepared for the energy that surrounded mixed bathing, and I wondered why anyone would want to share another's bath water. The only experience I had that cast any light on the subject was the memory of a Saturday night bathing ritual in drought-stricken Texas when all of our cousins were run through a communal bathtub to the embarrassment of the older girls who felt modesty was more important than saving water. When I finally discovered what was at stake, I realized that growing up in California really was different from growing up in Texas or Tennessee.

On reflection, the single most important thing I learned about church was that it was part of the social construct of our lives. It was the laboratory for living where we tested our sense of right and wrong. The theological dimensions of our life together was a veneer that was not very deep. We did not reach many people who were irreligious. We fine-tuned folk who were like us but had a few rough edges that needed to be rounded off. We baptized our own as children came of age, but we seldom baptized the children of others. A few husbands/wives found the faith in order to marry, but the heathen did not join our ranks, and we did not go looking for them.

Theology was for me a live notion because I was expected to preach. My training was modest. I was given a Bible and encouraged to read it. I was given a concordance so I could link together similar English words that appeared in texts. From the beginning, I was uncomfortable with the links so created. On one occasion I led a Wednesday night gathering over the rough roads of my sense of logic to a conclusion that was nailed down by a reference to scripture that turned out to read differently from the King James Version I was using. My conclusion shattered, I scurried from the pulpit overwhelmed by embarrassment and thought to myself, "Well, at least I will never do that again," but of course I did.

Our minister at the time was Glenn Wallace. He was of the Wallace clan well known in Church of Christ circles. He had come to us from the College Church in Abilene where he had been deemed too rough around the edges for a college crowd. One Sunday he put a wash rag on his head and imitated the Pope. Later near the end of the Vietnam war, he sent me a letter telling me of his disappointment in me for my opposition to the war. But that gets us a bit ahead of the story.

As I prepared to go off to ACU, Pepperdine College was in the throes of being reclaimed by Churches of Christ. M. Norvel Young was called by the Board to save the college, and he did so in the short run. Looking at the University today perched on the hills in Malibu, it is clear he did far more. He laid the foundation for a successful institution and forced those of us so inclined to think about what a church-related college might mean in the second half of the 20th century.

While this was going on, I was off to Abilene to learn about important things like mixed bathing, how one copes with plagues of locust, and the ethical implications of the absence of an ocean. On the horizon was the Cuban Missile Crisis, Vietnam, and the Civil Rights Movement, but we were largely unaware. That could not go on forever.

For me, it was a gradual dawning. I recognized how much I did not know. I was expected to achieve in all of my endeavors, but the bar was set pretty low. In high school I had been a leader and was successful with few setbacks; I served as President of the Student Body, and at Abilene, I became class president and then broke new ground by running twice for student body president and losing each time. I learned a lot about failing in those endeavors, but that was nothing compared to what I was learning in the classroom.

LeMoine Lewis, B. Frank Rhodes, Paul Rotenberry, James Culp, Keith Justice, Francis Churchill opened doors that I gladly walked through and while I am sure they would not have shared all the conclusions I have reached, I am confident they would acknowledge the importance of the journey because they believed that teaching was the task of revealing in the classroom what students needed to know if life was to be lived in a meaningful way.

My trajectory was an uncertain one. I came to ACC on an agriculture scholarship and quickly determined that unless one was born with land, a future in farming or ranching was unlikely. I graduated with a degree in History and Bible and had developed a desire to learn more about church history. Seminary seemed a logical goal, but by then, marriage was on the horizon, and while Jan Cothran finished her degree, I went to Pepperdine to complete an M.A. in American History. We married in May of 1964 and completed our degrees in August and headed off to Yale Divinity School. Jan began teaching in Wallingford, CT. The experience was life-changing for both of us.

LeMoine had suggested Yale to me and the dean of American Church historians, Sydney Ahlstrom, was on the faculty at Yale completing his *A Religious History of the American People* while teaching in the seminary. I was able to take courses downtown with C. Vann Woodward and Edmund Morgan in addition to honors work with Ahlstrom. The noted Luther scholar, Roland Bainton, had just retired but was still a presence on campus. Paul Minear taught New Testament, David Little was beginning his career, and Stanley Hauerwas was completing his graduate study. It was a heady time made even more so by the tides of the Civil Rights movement and the conversations going on around us.

When I went to Yale, I was still a sectarian. I had learned enough in Abilene to know that the emperor's clothes were tattered, but I still thought and lived in the bubble created by the Churches of Christ. Jimmy Allen at the New York World's Fair helped pierced the bubble by offering a defense of southern culture as part of a sermon that was offered to members of Churches of Christ gathered from across the eastern seaboard. It did not go over well.

More significantly, I was invited to speak about the Churches of Christ to a gathering at Disciples House on the Yale campus. Members of our congregation in Hamden were there to hear me speak the truth to the digressives and I took the high ground by emphasizing that we took the Bible seriously. Later over coffee the late Hiram Lester, then teaching Greek at Yale and on his way to a career at Bethany College, came up to me and quietly said that the Disciples took the Bible seriously as well. The scales dropped from my eyes.

Yale was profoundly important. The opportunity to live among other students preparing to serve churches I had been taught were fatally flawed was impossible to experience without coming to recognize your own denominational shortcomings. Then as if to drive home the point, Ira Y. Rice arrived at Yale to study Mandarin.

His coming was not a surprise. We had been assured that the Ira Rice we knew by reputation had changed, but he had not. He spent his New Haven year not going to class, but rather lifting the curtain on the heresy sweeping the Churches of Christ, and we were exhibit A in his three-book series called *Axe on the Root*.

He had come home to the U.S. and found the church he had known by his standards to be in a state of apostasy. The rest of his career until his death in 2001 was spent in the service of that notion. For me, the experience made it clear that the Biblicism that passed for an interpretative framework for Churches of Christ was fatally flawed. The slogans we proclaimed were always compromised by loudest voices in the conversation. There was no sense that the Holy Spirit was at work to moderate conclusions and no historical sense of where we had been to help us avoid extremes. That a voice like that of Ira Y. Rice could command a following was a reminder of the human nature of the church that should have taught us to lessen our judgments of those in other Christian communities.

The shattered state of the Restoration Movement is no worse, nor is it better than the shattered state of every other major religious tradition in America. Each has strong points and each has blind spots. In the aftermath of Rice, this was clear, but the challenge was to find a place to stand while working through the issues given to our generation. Many of my peers moved into other traditions where they felt it easier to use their talents on the issues they thought important. I chose to stay within the Churches of Christ and to work through outlets such as Mission Journal while working to make it easier for religious groups to flourish on campus in an increasingly secular age.

A healthy university brings together a diverse community working out questions of meaning and identity together in dialogue. Dimensions of identity include a range of markers that are in addition to the intellectual exercise that goes on in the classroom. The search for meaning in life is part of the process that dominates student lives. The process may well not end until life itself draws to a close.

Called in 2007 to be the Chaplain to the Institute offered me the chance to grow by learning and experiencing the religious lives of MIT students. My world view had been growing since with my Grandfather I had attended meetings in support of missions to Japan. Race awareness had been a constant byproduct of my experiences at Southwestern. Now I learned from Muslim students from Saudi Arabia, Buddhist monks from India, Jewish students from Brookline! The role I was asked to fill was in many ways not greatly different than the role I filled when I walked across the train tracks in Terrell and challenged the notion that there were no other Christians than those who looked and acted like us. My role was to listen and to ask questions.

My affection for the Bible and my love of Christ and his church has not waned, but I understand better what Krister Stendahl wrote some years ago:

> *For the longer I live, the less adequate and less useful become all those stifling distinctions between academy and church,*

faith and reason, the intellectual and the spiritual. There is such an interplay between those fabricated distinctions that one cannot live without the other.[2]

I am not going to try and untangle the distinctions. The objects of our affections are to be loved by heart and head. That has been my posture in pew and pulpit. I have experienced the extremes of piety run amuck, and the results of tradition accepted uncritically, so I engage in the conversation. That leads me to my hopes for the future of the Churches of Christ.

I believe that God is at work in our churches, so my suggestions are not for our effort alone, but that our efforts complement the work of God.

In the first place, I would hope that we might understand that the church is a living organism. We are all familiar with the idea that the members of the church make their contributions as parts of the body. We are not comfortable with the notion that the body renews itself and changes as it grows. We would like for it to be as we liked it best, but living entities change. We may not always be comfortable with change, but it is the nature of life. The church today is not as it was when I was a child; it is not like the church I read about in the early 19th century or in the first century. So long as it seeks to be the body of Christ doing the will of God, it is Christ's church. God is at work. We need to remember and believe that truth.

My second hope for the church is Church of Christ specific. We need to remember that the tradition we draw our identity from began as a unity movement. The confusion of sectarianism prompted the evangelists of the Restoration Movement to propose that by taking the Bible seriously we might take advantage of the blank slate of the American experience and find a way to tell the story of Jesus in a way that would present a more effective Christian witness. We have given that up for a defense of our tradition. From time to time, it is important to be reminded of the essential unity of those who name the name of Christ.

---

[2] Krister Stendahl, *Why I Love the Bible.*

We can start most effectively with those we share a wider tradition with. It is hard to undo the hurts of generations, but it is a task worth taking up.

Finally, when we have learned to present Christ in how we live and to teach his message as effectively as possible, we must recognize that we have done what we can do and it is time to seek to know the other by becoming as aware of the other as we demand they be of us. We cannot wash our hands and turn away. My life has been enriched by time spent with Buddhist monks, Jewish rabbis, Hindu Priests. I hope that Churches of Christ might become the best informed religious communities in our world. Given the tenor of our times, such a commitment might well set us apart from our peers, but I have no doubt that God would view our courage as exploring the mysteries of the Divine.

Looking Back
by Lynn Anderson

Let me take you back to Osijek, Croatia, circa February 1999. Peter, our Croatian friend, had arranged for a stranger to ride with us on our drive from Osijek to Zagreb. Just as were to climbing into the car, Peter introduced the stranger: "Lynn, meet my brother-in-law, Miroslav Volf." A few weeks earlier Christianity Today had published a cover picture of Miroslav Volf, as "one of the top seven Theologians of the 1990s." And I couldn't wait to pick his brain. After a bit, I asked a theological question, and Volf deflected it with a Croatian political joke. But my questions persisted, until Volf finally answered, "You know, I have no interest in discussing Theology…(long pause)…apart from Ministry." Then (after another brief silence) he added, "And I have no interest in discussing Ministry—apart from Theology." Yes! Volf's brief, cogent comment confirmed my long-held contention: Scholars and Pastors are all one team, *and we really do need each other*. Really!

My parents were baptized in 1936 when Mother was pregnant with me. So "church" has been central to my entire 80 years of life. But, we met in homes. I remember awakening early on Sunday morning, to the inviting aroma of unleavened bread baking in Mother's oven. Then I heard the pop of the lid being lifted from the jar of grape juice.

Soon the 25 members of our little church gathered in our dining room. We sang a few hymns. Then prayed. Then, with no preacher, we swapped insights from our various home Bible readings, partook of the Lord's Supper, and closed with a hymn. Then *all 25 of us* enjoyed lunch together. That too was "church."

Now, 70 years later, the church we "attend" has six campuses—with 10,000 attending. Our assemblies feature a Lucado sermon and a high-tech, contemporary praise extravaganza!

Oh yes, things *have definitely changed* in my 80 years of life: *The World has changed. The Church has changed. Lynn Anderson has changed.* Here are just a few glimpses—decade by decade.

THE 1950'S—BEGINNINGS

My "church memories" begin in rural Saskatchewan, right after WW II, secure in the circle of our tiny congregation. When I was 12, I won first place in a Province-wide "public speaking contest," and church folk began predicting that I would be a preacher. At the age of fourteen, I left home, for my high school years at a Christian boarding high-school—190 miles away—which provided frequent public speaking opportunities, often in chapel—even at church.

After High School, I was off to Freed-Hardeman College in far away Tennessee. The exotic south felt like "living in a storybook." But our teachers were "of their time and place" on race and theology. Nevertheless, I remember them as kind-hearted Mentors who taught us to love the Bible and *The Church*. I found Carolyn there too.

During college years I preached somewhere every Sunday. However, my natural "speaking gift" enabled laziness, and I plagiarized more sermons than I prepared. And I scraped by at school, on *"scholastic probation"* the first two years.

However, things began to change in 1957 when Carolyn and I married and transferred to Harding. Marriage and a regular preaching appointment every-Sunday-at-Tupelo made me feel more adult. But I was 21 and a "cocky" Freed Hardeman transfer, amused by heckling those "liberal Harding Professors," like Dr. Jim, who taught my American Literature class. I blush to recall my relentless disrespect those first two days. Then, after class the second day, Dr. Jim quietly asked me, "Lynn, *who talked you into going to college?"* I was stunned. "Actually, no one," I sputtered. (In retrospect, I had assumed a diploma was the ticket to "authentic preacher-hood"—but I hadn't really expected to *learn* anything much—preaching was just "making speeches.")

Dr. Jim continued, "You don't need a college degree to be a worthwhile human being. My advice? Skip College—unless you, yourself, really want to learn. Otherwise, college is a waste of your money." Then, he added, "But you need to decide right away! Because, if you stay much longer, college may awaken your intellectual curiosity. And if that happens, you'll never be able to turn back."

As Dr. Jim walked away, I realized it was already too late! This good man had just nudged me toward a life-transforming decision. I never *have* been able to turn back. An insatiable curiosity has continually stretched my faith and made me a life-long student. In 1958 our eldest daughter, Michele, was born.

MEMPHIS

The fall of 1959, we moved to Memphis to begin graduate studies. This opened new worlds, but also raised a new question: "Why was my theology working for everybody else, but not for me?' And it came as a real shock when I discover that "my *theology" didn't seem to fit other souls either.* That jolt came the last night of a Revival in rural Missouri. A non-churched woman had attended every night, children in tow, leaving her unemployed, alcoholic husband at home. This tiny woman had few teeth left but still chewed tobacco. And I doubt she could read. But she listened intently.

The final night I found my full-throated hell-fire and brimstone voice. While I scorched the pews with guilt, she hung on every word. Afterword, as she shook my hand, her lip quivered. And she spoke her heart, "you know what preacher. I shore am glad I ain't a Christian. It's *tough enough just being a sinner like me."* For a moment, I hoped she was joking. But *No, she wasn't*. My mind flashed back through the week. Night after night, this woman sat listening for some Gospel—some Good News. But, what that troubled soul heard all week was anything but good news!

I drove away, promising God that I would never preach that way again. And I set out in pursuit of a healthier, more hopeful message.

This was timely, because, that year at Harding Grad, we began learning *about how* to think, not just *what* to think. Also, that year, I met Charles Coil, who showed me *how to think about persons.* And showed me what love *looks like* day after day, in a local church. So in the fall of 1960, we moved to British Columbia, Canada to help plant a church in Salmon Arm, in a small town in the mountains.

THE 1960'S

The previous five years had acculturated me to rural Bible Belt Religious life. But B. C. people were far more secular than Bible Belt people. Also, in the South, I had preached mostly to kind country folk who loved to encourage their "boy preachers." But, our Salmon Arm church started with just eight people who didn't know or like each other very much. So with no gallery of affirming fans, I was forced to face my real self; and fly solo into a blizzard of questions and doubts. My paramount question was, "Will this Bible Belt version of the Restoration Movement' work' in Western Canada?"

In Canada, our Restoration Tribe was too small to afford the luxury of division, so churches of Christ, Independent Christian churches and Disciples of Christ, looked to each other for fellowship. This nudged me to further deconstruct my "pattern hermeneutic." Questions persisted. But we soldiered on four years and left behind a fledgling church—which is still there. Also, we took with us two more children, Debbie and Jon, born in Salmon Arm.

LEPANTO AND MEMPHIS

We spent 1964-65 back in Memphis to finish the M. Div. However, I also hoped to find a resolution for my Questions. I preached in Lepanto, Arkansas, that year and drove to Memphis for classes—and organized people to join us for our next B. C. church plant. And I actually finished my Master's Thesis! Best of all, those supportive professors sent us back to Kelowna, B. C. with a much healthier message and a greatly improved state of emotional well-being.

KELOWNA, B. C., 1965—1971

Kelowna was much larger City. The 60's revolution drew Hippies from everywhere to Kelowna's sunny beaches, where they ignored institutions and values, and celebrated "Freedom" with drugs, sex, and rock n' roll.

Carolyn and I relished another season of life, packed with exciting new ministry opportunities. I joined the Ministerial Association for conversation with other Christian Tribes. And a Catholic Priest became my closest companion on the inward journey. In fact, his counsel may have saved my ministry. I also found surprising allies outside the Church Bubble. I played hockey with a radio DJ who taught me how to write radio spots. A newspaper editor taught me "how things work in this town."

These Kelowna years stretched my theological foundations and improved my preaching and ministry methods exponentially. Consequently, by 1969, I saw myself heading where our Bible Belt supporters likely wouldn't want to go. I felt duplicitous. But, I also began to question whether my gifts were best suited for church planting? I begged God for answers.

THE 1970'S – HIGHLAND AND ACU

Answers came in a phone call from Abilene, Texas. Long story short: the summer of 1971 we left our Kelowna friends—and took with us our 4 children (second son, Christopher, was born in Kelowna)—and headed south to the pulpit of the Highland church of Christ; from cool Canadian Rockies to hot Texas plains. And from a church of 40-50 folks in a rented hall to a church of nearly 2,000 members, and a nationwide profile, in a small city of under 100,000.

The '60s had radically changed the American landscape. By the 70's the icons of hope, the Kennedys and Martin Luther King were dead. So were Camelot and Aquarius. America was in a funk. Churches across the nation languished at a crossroads, feeling irrelevant and in decline. But Highland people seemed to care and were open to change.

We soon realized that the word "change" easily awakens the malevolent forces of national church politics. Somehow I found myself in the middle of controversy. And two years into the job, I got myself fired! Then *rehired a week later.* The second time I got to stay 17 more years.

During those years, the church flourished—and I personally grew—within that. Toward the end of our Highland tenure, I finally completed a Doctor of Ministry degree. However, before that, the Highland shepherds had immeasurably deepened our lives: We escaped legalism and sectarianism together. We laughed and cried together. And we pursued God together.

Also, God afforded me the opportunity to work side by side with transformational staff colleagues, two of whom were David Lewis and David Wray. We prayed Psalms together. And pursued contemplative life-paths, together. And together *"ran toward the light."* But the best growing for Carolyn and me came from rearing our four beloved children, in whom we are well pleased.

And doors of ministry continued to open. ACU invited me to teach a Ministry course once a year as an adjunct. Also each year I mentored circles of ministry student interns. And circles of young married marketplace men. Radio spots opened doors in the community, and platforms at graduations, civic organizations—and the pulpits of numerous churches beyond our "Tribe."

But of all the Highland accomplishments, the two which give me the most satisfaction: Helping position churches of Christ in a more positive light among the Abilene religious community, and helping our elders see themselves as a circle of shepherds doing soul-care rather than as a board of directors making decisions.

By the late '80s, the Highland church and the Anderson family were becoming too comfortable with each other. I felt I was beginning to coast, the church seemed happy to coast, and I feared we might happily decline into oblivion together.

Also, I felt pulled away from Abilene more and more—by pleas for help from ministers and elders struggling to lead churches in chaotic, changing times. As these invitations multiplied, my heart's first priority gradually shifted away from Highland toward those struggling

Church leaders. Carolyn and I woke up one morning and realized we were empty nesters—and free to live more peripatetic lives.

So, in 1990, I resigned from Highland, and we moved immediately to Dallas to start a full-time ministry to Christian Leaders on their turf.

THE 1990's—DALLAS

By 1990, the Baby Boomer generation emerged as adults, partly as a backlash against the flower children of the '60s, and the funk of the '70s. Boomer was the demographic *"Pig in the Python;"* the largest age group ever to move through American life in one generation. And, the best-educated and wealthiest generation. Boomers felt entitled: and the country saw them as the generation that could fix everything.

By the 1990's Dallas was a Boomer-Mecca. And Preston Road church of Christ was one of the Boomer Believer gathering points. After a year doing Seminars and research, we accepted the preaching role at Preston Road—conditionally, "For no more than 5 years." But I also moonlighted at organizing our Christian Leader care upstart, called "Hope Network Ministries."

With our children grown and gone, a big part of "who we are" belonged to the past. And we soon learned that credibility doesn't transfer.

In Abilene, I had learned a new way to preach—like a chaplain. And new ways to lead: I had adapted to academic and therapist type of people, who want to "talk things through." But Preston Road was an affluent church, full of attorneys, CEO's, entrepreneurs who all wanted to "get things done."

Nevertheless, in a few short years, we became attached to the Preston Road people and left a big part of our hearts there too. In fact, several leaders from Preston Road have been Hope Network board members—two are still on the board today. However, in 1996, at the end of our 5-year agreement, I resigned from Preston Road to go full time with Hope Network Ministries.

Staying The Course

2000–2017 San Antonio

In 2001 we moved Hope Network to San Antonio to be nearer our family. During our first decade here, Hope Network kept me on the road most weekends.

Eight years ago, at age 72, I was flying high, fully engaged in ministry. But one day, an oncologist looked me in the eye and said, "Sir, You have lung cancer." Then came surgery. Then 18 months of aggressive treatment.

When it became obvious that we could no longer sustain the pace, we chose Jon Mullican and Grady King to lead Hope Network, and handed the leadership over to them, and I resigned as President, and I semi-retired. However, we will always minister peace, as God brings opportunity and strength.

By God's grace nearly 3 years ago, I passed the magic 5 years of Remission. Only the aftermath lingers—but the journey brings more changes.

I don't want to go there again. And, I don't believe God gave me cancer. But I am unspeakably thankful that He allowed me to walk this cancer pathway, because of what He is teaching me through it. Most importantly, He is teaching me to accept my own powerlessness. I feel He has moved my heart from Warrior to Lamp.

Remember the day King David got fired? Another battle broke out and King David, the old warrior buckled on his sword—once more—and headed for the action. However, by this time, David was well along in years, and he had lost a step or two. A young Philistine took advantage and was about to take King David down. Then Abishai came to the old man's rescue and dispatched the Philistine. "Then David's men swore to him, saying, "Never again will you go out with us to battle [sad words—until we read the last half of the sentence] "so that the *lamp of Israel will not be extinguished*" (2 Samuel 21:17).

David's men sent him home from battle. But not because he was *useless*. Quite the contrary; they sent him home *because he was indispensable*. He was far more valuable as a *Lamp;* spreading light and hope at the heart of the kingdom, than as *Sword Swinger* at its fringes.

Of course, I make no claim to be the source of light and hope for the people of God. But from over here in this part of life, I see things differently.

Richard Rohr's book, *Falling Upward* (about the second half of life), started me actually writing down a list of ways that "second half" eyes see the World:

Lamps have discovered that things, which used to matter to us, don't anymore. *Some Warriors don't "get" this, and think the Lamp has gone limp, or liberal or lukewarm. Warriors are drawn to absolutes; short black and white answers.*

Lamps are drawn to Mystery, paradox, even ambiguity. Obsessing over "getting it right" blocks out *Wonder.*

Lamps discover that the most significant "lamping" flows out of quietness. Lamps read a Bigger Bible. If one doesn't give up on the Bible but keeps reading it over and over, one will eventually find him or her self-listening to a bigger Bible.

I am definitely hearing a different Bible now, than the one I read in the early days. That Bible sounded like a Constitution. Or a book of case law. Like a psychology text. A science book and a history tome. A book of facts.

But the Bible I read now sounds so much richer. And I take it much more seriously. I hear a Grand Narrative of God and Humankind, told by "many voices," that seem, at times, to contradict one another, but taken all together, can unfold a compelling, and magnificent and nuanced Story. A story of mystery, and paradox, sometimes even ambiguity—and Wonder.

These days I listen and watch for *Wonder*!

So my word from an old preacher that stumbled into a company of young theologians: "Wherever you go, whatever you do, *don't forget to watch for Wonder.*"

LOOKING AHEAD

Of course, no one can predict the future. But trends indicate that Churches in the United States will move further away from current denominational maps and further polarize along political and theological lines. However, among mainstream churches of Christ, although some are flourishing, many are searching for clearer identity. I believe the mega-church wave will crest. And, experimental church formats will likely multiply in shapes far beyond my imagination.

Whatever the church looks like in the century ahead *the Kingdom of God* will continue to flourish—but to shift. Already, the geographical locus of the Christian faith is rapidly shifting from the United States and Europe to Africa, Asia, and Latin America. From North to South, from white to color. Hope lies ahead.

But ahead also lies a massive challenge. Humankind is lethally *polarized* over a juggernaut of loaded issues. Research by Psychologist Jonathan Haidt poses a daunting possibility.[1] Haidt notes that every subculture lives inside its own narrative. But regardless of the narrative in which one lives, when confronted with a strong idea that challenges one's narrative all cultures instinctively react in the same way: First, "I" rally "facts" that prove the "other" is wrong. Second, "I" marshals "facts" that prove "I'm" right. Third, since "other" refuses to see that "I" am right, and "other" is wrong, then "other" is either stupid or evil. Fourth, therefore "I" must reject out of hand all new information that comes from outside my Narrative.

If Haidt is right about this, collaborating toward a better future seems impossible. Maybe, but *my hope is that Kingdom people may be best positioned to help humankind move past this.* Perhaps a community of "blessed peacemakers" can at least help *change the conversation* from polarization to collaboration. And the first step may be to stop "telling" and start "listening."

Dr. Jerry Taylor sees a Nation polarized by fear.[2] One "pole" fears *extinction.* And seeks to protect its position by purifying "our" gene pool – and by gathering the wealth and power into "our" hands. The other "pole" fears *genocide,* and seeks to protect its survival through

---

[1] Haidt, Jonathan, *The Righteous Mind: Why Good People are Divided by Politics and Religion.* Random House, 2012.

[2] In conversation, April 17, 2017.

"power in numbers," by expanding the gene pool and winning the birth-rate race—and sharing earned wealth with all who help earn it.

Taylor offers at least one possible solution—though it sounds radical: his solution is *"Silence!"* He gathers small *communities* of 10-12 persons from significantly differing narratives (world views, ethnicities, and ideologies, etc.) to simply *be Quiet! Be quiet together, learning to listen to God and to each other.* In this way understanding and mutual trust could grow, until "us" and "other" can collaborate toward a better future. Sounds fanciful, yes. But it is the DNA of the church; it is the way Jesus started His "movement." Could one path to the future run through the past?

Roads More Traveled
by Tom Olbricht

I never perceived myself as unique—one of a kind. I may admit to being a legend in my own mind, but I readily excuse those who differ. My story doesn't need telling again. I have already adequately explained my past in *Hearing God's Voice: My Life with Scriptures in Churches of Christ* (ACU Press, 1996); *Reflections on My Life in the Kingdom and the Academy* (Eugene, OR: Wipf and Stock, 2012); and *Missouri Memories 1934-1947* (Eugene, OR: Wipf and Stock, 2016). In this essay, I reminisce on the roads I have traveled. Many have left tread marks on the same asphalt. We continue down the roads more traveled. I will focus on (1) capabilities and environment, (2) my religious life, (3) education, and end with (4) possible destinations for the roads ahead.

(1) Capabilities and environment

I believe that humans turn out the way they do because of their capabilities and the environment. I also believe that life is modified by the roads selected for travel. My mother, Agnes Taylor Olbricht came from a healthy family. Some of our patriarchs lived into their nineties. They were Scots-Irish and French and migrated to the United States in the eighteenth century. My father's family emigrated from Germany after the Civil War. They too possessed long-lasting DNA. I was rigorous in physique but not too well coordinated, so I tended not to excel in sports. My skills in manual labor were impressive. In the routines of bailing and stacking hay and later in operating a capper in a California

Packing plant in DeKalb, Illinois, I was the superior on the production line; able to vacuum lift above 300 filled cans a minute into a metal tray for transferring to the cooker. My construction boss for DeKalb AG put me to work whenever I was available because of my physical skills, even after I took up graduate studies at the University of Iowa.

I am reluctant to talk about my intellectual skills because I later met so many whose capabilities were superior to mine. I was known to have an exceptional memory and healthy eyes. I was informed by the local Methodist minister, who sought information about his son, that I had the highest IQ score of anyone one in our high school of 250 students. But I paled in comparison with some of my later students who made perfect scores on the GRE. Physically and mentally, I had the capability for various occupations. I was asked to manage a national religious radio program. When I was fifty some friends who owned a plastics molding company in New England tried their best to employ me as president of their company. I told them that working with outstanding students came first.

It might appear that my intellectual environment determined the roads I traveled. My relatives, however, weren't bookish except for my mother. They were well informed. They read daily and weekly newspapers and listened each day to noonday and nighttime news. Otherwise, they seldom read even though several were teachers. Many of my relatives were college educated, which was unusual for the time and place. They were teachers, farmers, business proprietors, managers, and salespersons. If they side-stepped college, they studied at technical schools and during World War II were taught various skills by the military. My mother, however, was a reader and writer for women's religious journals. She encouraged her children to read. Because of my parsimonious athletic skills, I turned to reading even though I was discouraged by my father and some of the other relatives. They thought I should be outside. I read numerous religious books, especially those of Lloyd C. Douglas. I turned out to be a reader and writer, but as an adult focused on matters pertaining to the scriptures.

Probably what contributed most from my environment, however, was the relentless energy of my forbears. Even as an eighty-year-old, my German grandfather spent full days in farm activities. When the weather threatened, he turned to making wurst, that is, German sausages, as well as processing other farm products. He had been trained as a tanner and around on the inside walls of the barn were animal hides of various sorts. My grandfather Taylor was normally out of the house by seven A. M. so as to open up the store for people on their way to work. He kept the store open until eight at night. He kept a full calendar day in and day out with rarely a break. When I stayed with my grandparents, I helped during the busy hours. My uncle Cleo, with whom I stayed and attended high school, was always at work doing something. His main position was as a vocational agriculture teacher at Alton High School. By the time I arrived to help him, he had bought a thousand-acre plot of land on which he grazed about a hundred cows. He also had a hundred angora goats. Much of the "ranch" was covered with scrub oak trees. The goats inhibited the growth of the oaks or at least ate of the lower parts so that more grass was available. We also sheared the goats and sold the wool. At one time we milked about twenty cows and delivered bottled milk to the residents of the town. We were up at six and normally did not eat "supper" until after seven at night. Sometimes when the prices were right, my uncle bought feeder cattle and hogs and trucked them to farmers in northern Missouri where more corn and other grains were available to feed them out. We kept busy rain or shine.

(2) Religious Life

Most of what I recall from early years focused on religion and the church. My mother showed up at church whenever the doors opened. When we had summer Gospel Meetings, she and my siblings attended every morning and night service. On her side of the family, I was a fourth generation restorationist. My great-grandfather, John Moody Taylor and his wife Amy Anthum Waits Taylor, were baptized at the same time in northwestern Alabama before the Civil War. According to family traditions, they had heard the famous evangelist T. B. Larimore. My grandfather, T. Shelt Taylor, through his middle years, was a church leader and Bible teacher. He owned a convenience store-gas station, and when no customers were around he read the Bible. He loved to argue with preachers over favorite conclusions of his, for example, that the Apostles were set, not baptized, into the church.

I started seriously considering baptism when I was ten. I was rather reticent before a crowd and kept putting it off until I was sixteen. I had heard the meeting sermons many times from G. K. Wallace and others. They declared that the right name for the church is church of Christ; that Jesus is head of the church; and that the church is led by elders and deacons. They were especially insistent that the way to salvation is hearing, believing, repenting, confessing, and being baptized by immersion. I thought some of this teaching was mechanistic but nevertheless true. Before I was baptized, Reuel Lemmons held a meeting at Mammoth Spring, Arkansas, where we attended. I liked his preaching better. He spoke more of the dedicated religious life. I also got to hear Boyd Morgan from Northeastern Arkansas. He often took his sermons from the gospels and the parables. These sentiments rang true for me as to how a Christian should live. I finally got up the nerve to respond to the invitation. My two brothers Glenn and Owen responded at the same time along with a cousin Don Beatty. I didn't take this new road lightly. I decided to give it my best. I even started contributing from my own bank account more than I ever anticipated.

In the fall of 1947, I entered Harding College as a freshman. My sister Nedra was already there. My mother especially encouraged me to go to Harding. She told me that if I went to the University of Missouri to study agriculture as I intended, my dad wouldn't help me, but he would if I went to Harding at least two years. I found the religious climate at Harding much different. The emphasis was on a heartfelt religion. We often sang before a service, "Into my heart, into my heart, come into my heart Lord Jesus. Come in today, come in to stay, come into my heart Lord Jesus." Or "My Jesus I love thee I know thou art mine." We never sang such songs at our home church. Before long, I made up my mind to give a short devotional talk at a college gathering especially designed for that purpose. I had a bad case of stage fright, but I made it through with the commendation of my peers. I had heard enough sermons that I had plenty of models from which to draw. I was especially influenced to consider at least being a teacher in the churches by being around Andy T. Ritchie, Jr. I took my first year of Bible classes with him. I didn't talk with him much, but his own devotion impressed me deeply.

In January of 1948, encouraged by friends who drove out of Searcy on Sunday by the carload to preach, I decided to do so myself. My first sermons were preached near Conway, then east of Newport and later with another friend north of Pocahontas. I also preached a few times near my home in Thayer, Missouri. I preached to the east at Jeff, Missouri, where I had several Taylor and Olbricht relatives. My mother made an appointment for me to preach at English Bluff, Arkansas, where even more relatives lived. But though my mother made me try every known old wives' remedy, I couldn't preach because of a cold and hoarseness. I also preached at Brandsville, Missouri, toward West Plains and Lanton, Missouri, west of Thayer.

My perspectives on the nature of the church and its growth took a quantum leap in these years. I became acquainted with Christians from all over the United States and from some foreign countries. Many important preachers visited the campus, and I heard a number of different approaches to topics and preaching style. I basked in this variety. I met several persons my age who anticipated planting churches in Japan, Africa, and Europe. The time was not too long after World War II. Our leaders, some of whom had served in distant countries during the war, were determined to go into all the world to proclaim the Biblical faith. I was caught up in a new vision as to the prospect to promulgate New Testament Christianity.

During the spring term of 1948 Don Horn, a good friend, talked me into going with him to DeKalb, Illinois, where his brother lived, and help start a congregation. I would work for California Packing Company, canning peas and corn; and for DeKalb Ag, detasseling corn. My relatives weren't too excited about the undertaking, but as long as the money was good, they thought it was a good opportunity to be involved in church work. Andy T. Ritchie was directing campaigns in the northeast during those years and James D. Willeford who preached for the congregation in Madison, Wisconsin, kept writing, trying to get him to bring a campaign to Madison. Ritchie had already scheduled his summer, but he encouraged anyone interested to help with the work in Madison. I took a Greyhound to Madison and met Dorothy for the first time. We knocked doors together. I was impressed with her boldness. Three years later, we married in Madison. Not only was I set for a mate for at least the next 65 years, she greatly encouraged me to preach. Willeford, who shared a vision with James Walter Nichols for a national radio program, "The Herald of Truth," became our advisor and supporter.

    I was soon aware that the religious climate in DeKalb was different from the one in which I grew up. Various liberal churches dotted the landscape, but because of Wheaton College and Moody Bible Institute, there were also numerous fundamentalists. That first summer we spent our extra time locating members of churches of Christ who had moved into the area. Most of them came from Black Rock, Arkansas, Don's hometown, Danville, Kentucky (some of these being from conservative Christian Churches), and from Greenville, Tennessee. We left Dekalb that summer with about 25 persons meeting on Sunday afternoons. I decided to go back to DeKalb the next summer. My brothers Glenn and Owen accompanied me. They worked for California Packing Company and I with the DeKalb Ag construction crew.

    In the meantime, during the school year R. E. Van Tassell, the Rockford, Illinois, preacher came to DeKalb on Sunday afternoon. He was good at finding former church of Christ members who didn't attend church. We now had about 40 persons meeting regularly in a rented hall on the second floor in downtown DeKalb. The elders and Van Tassell started talking to me about moving to DeKalb, attending Northern Illinois State Teacher's College and preaching for the congregation in DeKalb. This had some appeal because I had decided that in addition to being a rancher on my father's homestead in western Nebraska, I would plant congregations. I decided to take a degree in speech at Northern, then complete a degree in agriculture from the University of Missouri. But the more I preached, the more I liked it so as my senior year rolled around I had decided that I wanted to teach homiletics. I heard W. B. West of Harding say that the ideal teacher of homiletics had a B. D. from a seminary and a Ph. D. in speech. Being encouraged by teachers and by various preachers I decided, however audacious it sounds, to attain these two degrees which entailed a minimum six years of graduate courses.

Another preacher, James P. Sanders who was blind, made a deep impression. His wife traveled with him wherever he went. He possessed a B. D. from the seminary at Vanderbilt. He also had acquired an M.Th. from Yale Divinity School. He had a well-modulated resonate voice and which, when needed, conveyed deep emotion. In about two years the congregation in Rockford increased from 150 attendees to above 400. He focused on the need of compassion for widows and orphans and the poor. He employed texts, especially from the Old Testament prophets I seldom heard in sermons. He came to DeKalb that fall and preached a series of sermons. We designated them "series" because people of the area were not familiar with the term "Gospel Meeting." We tried to use language that would convey the proper idea to the people of Northern Illinois. In our advertizing, we gave great emphasis to the undenominational character of our preaching. We learned, however, that undenominational to people from independent churches of the region did not convey an emphasis on clear Bible teaching, but rather that our church was not a part of any group of churches or denominations which from their perspective we were. It was from these experiences that I became interested in tailoring a language that resonated with the understandings in the minds of those reading or listening.

I was busy in the spring of 1951 taking courses, student teaching in the local high school, debating on the University team, recording all this in a daily journal for a class and preparing to graduate, get married and make arrangements for what I would do next. I wanted to go to seminary and work on a B. D. Because of the influence of James A. Warren and others of our preachers who attended McCormick Theological Seminary in Chicago and because the McCormick approach was conventional and toward conservative, I wanted to attend McCormick. I asked various preachers in the Chicago area if they knew of one of our churches looking for a minister. They didn't know of any. Then I heard that the church in Iowa City was looking for a preacher. They would be open for me to work on a graduate degree at the University of Iowa. Some of my Northern Illinois speech professors who had obtained their Ph.D. at Iowa encouraged me to apply. I drove to Iowa City to talk with leaders of the congregation, some of the most committed ones being women. They said I could come and preach, but they wanted to bank all their money in order to buy a lot and build a building. They, therefore, didn't plan to give me any salary. I talked over the situation with James Willeford and he told me he thought he could find some money by way of support. It turned out that he had strong ties with a congregation in Haleyville, Alabama, and three members there who were involved in a car dealership made a commitment to send me $120 per month. We decided that with what Dorothy made we could survive. She worked as a desk clerk for a cleaner in town. It wasn't long before she became pregnant and we no longer had that income, but I made additional money as a teaching assistant at the university and one summer sold insurance to Iowa farmers in the region of Sigourney, Iowa. With some help with food from the farm of Dorothy's parents, we survived.

(3) Education

My graduate education contributed immeasurably to what I hoped to attain. But after undergraduate school, the additional graduate courses did not deter my goal of helping train preachers. I focused on church history and preaching. I took courses on Greek and Roman history and American orators. In all these courses, I focused on religious leaders and speakers. I decided to write my dissertation on the sermons of Basil the Great. I was encouraged by my teachers to do so. I took several hours of Greek in the classics department so as to read the sermons in Greek. I was greatly impressed by A. Craig Baird of national acclaim. He was one of the American founders of Speech studies. He was especially interested in preaching. He himself acquired a B.D. degree from Union Theological Seminary in 1912. He encouraged me in whatever way he could.

After teaching speech at Iowa, Harding, and the University of Dubuque I sought to attend Union Theological Seminary in the view of some the best seminary in the United States with Reinhold Niebuhr, John Knox, Paul Tillich, Cyril Richardson, and John Bennett as professors. I was admitted with a full scholarship, but I needed to job so as to support Dorothy and our four children. I found out from Everett Ferguson, who was going to Northeast Christian as Dean, that Pat Harrell was also leaving for Villanova and the Natick, Massachusetts, congregation where he preached was looking for a minister. At the recommendation of J. Harold Thomas, who did not know me, they offered me the job, sight unseen. It was a fortuitous turn of events, or shall we say providential, because the congregation owned a preacher's house suitable for a family of six. I immediately applied to Harvard Divinity School, where I was admitted and given a partial tuition scholarship. The impact of G. Ernest Wright, who taught Old Testament, was perhaps more influential than any teacher. The result was that when I was invited to teach Old Testament at Abilene Christian until they found someone with that specialty, I felt somewhat prepared. But then, because of the needs at ACU, I took up the teaching of Biblical theology, also a major interest of Wright and it became my focus. I was influenced in my outlooks on New Testament theology by Krister Stendahl at Harvard Divinity School and long conversations with Abraham J. Malherbe as to the centers of New Testament theology. Malherbe pointed me to such British authors as C. H. Dodd, Vincent Taylor, A. M. Hunter, and from the continent Oscar Cullmann. It was a solid education for the roads I sought to travel.

The Roads Ahead

If I read Romans 9-11 correctly, God is not yet through with his special people, Israel. God is long-suffering and he is still at work bringing the peoples at the ends of the earth into his kingdom. Similarly, I believe that God is not yet through with people from churches of Christ.

At various times in our history, we have had leaders who concluded that should humans plan and dedicate their lives to the task they could convert the world in one generation. I always thought these claims extravagant. The argument was that the first-century church accomplished as much, and we should get busy and accomplish the same. But this isn't an accurate depiction of the growth of early Christianity. Furthermore, while I believe that Christians are to go into all the world telling the good news night and day as did Paul, nevertheless the final outcome depends upon divine intent and action. God is not yet through with churches of Christ because he anticipates that they will yet arise from their lethargy and make their marks to the ends of the earth. It will come about rather because God moves so as to accomplish his determined ends. We need to follow the paths wherever He leads.

The history of Christendom is made up of renewed efforts to bring the world into the Kingdom. New directions resulted from the ministries of John Hus, William Tyndale, and Girolamo Savonarola. Redirections were empowered anew in the reforms of Luther, Calvin, and Zwingli. Religious awakenings rocked America; the first awakening engulfed Jonathan Edwards in the 1740s; the second great awakening in Kentucky early in the 1800s had Barton W. Stone as one of the chief leaders. Dwight Moody and Billy Sunday were at the forefront of another awakening and after World War II church life was renewed across the land as the result of the crusades of Billy Graham. Those surrounding Alexander Campbell engendered another sort of renewal having to do with the proclamation of the facts of the Gospel.

Sometimes we have to wait for divine forces to clear the paths so that people are eager to re-enter roads more traveled. We have this hope that they will discover the old paths anew. We anticipate a new age of empiricism and a new appreciation of orthodoxy. We need to be prepared and ready for it when it arrives.

For there is still a vision for the appointed time; it speaks of the end, and does not lie. If it seems to tarry, wait for it; it will surely come, it will not delay...but the righteous live by their faith [faithfulness]. Habakkuk 2:3-4 (NRSV)

Sing On
by Carolyn Hunter

Jesus Loves Me, This I Know...

I was born into the Berry family in Oklahoma City. I have two older sisters. We are in our eighties now, and all three of the "Berry Girls" have been members of the Church of Christ throughout their lives.

When I was a baby, our mother, whose family had been long-time Church of Christ members, worshiped with a new congregation, Culbertson Heights. During my elementary school years, John Banister preached there, and the church's very influential elder was Frank Winters, who led singing. When he spoke, we could count on the message being about love. During my growing up, K.C. Moser filled the pulpit at times when the regular minister was away. I knew that he was a somewhat controversial figure, and I was later to learn that he was an important thinker in the Stone-Campbell movement.

My father was a regular attender, but he had not become a member of the church until I was about 5 years old. His father was a Methodist preacher and my dad's large family had moved from one town to another every two or four years in Indian Territory/Oklahoma throughout his youth. They arrived in Wayne, Oklahoma, when he was about fifteen. He and my mother, Rhea Billingsley, graduated from High School there and went on to the University of Oklahoma.

My dad told me that to be a full member of the Methodist church of his youth, it was necessary to have a highly emotional conversion experience. He never had that experience. When he attended the Church of Christ with my mother and learned there that being saved and becoming a church member involved a rational series of steps, he was able to fulfill that requirement.

So in my family, emotion-filled religious life or emotion-directed personal life was suspect. We valued stoicism and privacy in our interactions. That's why you'll find as this memoir unfolds that it will not include the exciting, really terrible things that I've done. Anyhow, the Billingsley/Berry bunch were Campbellites rather than Stoneites. But for me, there has always been a rhythm of emotion underneath the intellectual. The emotion of religious life was suspended in the music of the church. We were good restorationists and we sang, sans instrument, to each other in psalms and hymns and spiritual songs and we did make melody in our hearts.

We went to church services three times a week. I listened and I was baptized when I was 12 after several years of feeling guilty. Shortly after that, John Banister and his family headed for Dallas, and George Bailey came to preach at Culbertson Heights. George died in 2017, and his and Ela Beth's surviving son, Philip, and I remain good friends. Although I thought these preachers knew more than I did, and I accepted their authority, at our dinner table conversations we evaluated and criticized what we had heard at church. My mother kept a close check on the grammar we heard from the pulpit. So there was some tension between church authority figures and individual interpretations and styles. There was definitely a premium on learning, on understanding and rightly dividing the word of truth.

My most influential class teacher was Mary Brown. There were probably six or eight kids my age at Culbertson Heights. Mary had a big, warm, fun-loving personality and she invested Bible stories with drama. Our classes met in the basement of the church. Our classroom did have a window below ground in a window well. It was probably a Vacation Bible School class that I remember the best. Usually the children were treated to an ice cream party, but one year the decree came down from above that there wouldn't be refreshments that year. So, we went dutifully to class, disappointed but resigned. Mary opened the grubby window and boosted Jerry Young up to street level and sent him to her car for punch and cookies. Our class had a party in secret. A communion of seven year olds. Here's a woman who broke the rules for the sake of the children she taught, and it's significant that that's the image that remains with me of a memorable Bible class.

I've two other stories from childhood that help to illuminate the forces that have shaped me.

I had the same 1st grade teacher as my sisters. The oldest of us, Maurine, whose career was as a music and elementary teacher, came home from first grade and taught her younger sister, Paula, to read. So when I was to follow Paula to Miss Kay's 1st grade class four years later, Miss Kays told my mother not to let anyone teach me to read. She wanted to do it. So I went to first grade ready to learn. In December, Miss Kays called me to her desk one day and asked me to read to her from a little book. In the book was the story of the birth of Jesus. So I read to her, whipping out "Jerusalem" and "Bethlehem" and "Herod" with no problem. I overheard her telling someone that she had taught only a very few children who could read that book. I suppose she was taking credit, but it was the Sunday School lessons that gave me the background to feature as a star reader for her. I think herein is a paradigm that continued throughout my academic career. My religious upbringing made me an attentive student of what was written in the Bible. Then that kind of attention to words and meanings and signifiers pushed me to examine other literature seriously and studiously.

My third childhood story takes me back to kindergarten. I started to Harmony School when I was five. Among the things that kindergarteners did then was to give a Christmas play for the school. I was cast as Mrs. Santa. You might think that Santa would be the leading character, but in this script, the Mrs. Santa got top billing. Here's the plot: Santa himself was incompetent. He went off with his reindeer but left the toys for 3 children behind. So Mrs. Santa saved the holiday by going out herself and delivering the gifts to the neglected children. As I look at this plot more than 75 years later, it seems to me that the seeds of a feminist philosophy may have been implanted along with the knowledge that you can get a real rush when people applaud for you. Carolyn the Actor was created. Through her the emotions of others are perceived and experienced and communicated.

How Shall the Young Secure Their Hearts…

By my Junior High years I had absorbed the idea at church that other religious groups were wrong. We knew this from our careful study and rational deductions. And I knew from experience that performing was delightful.

On graduating from High School, I didn't know what I wanted to do in the future. So here you have a person finishing High School. The grades are topnotch. The individual is deeply embedded in the church. There's a gift for languages. The main activities in Junior High and High School have been forensics and drama. This person is smart enough to succeed as a Biblical scholar. Now, I wonder what profession these talents and proclivities seem to fit? Preaching, right? But the idea never entered my head. I didn't have any insight into such a possibility.

Lord We Come Before Thee Now…In Thine Own Appointed Way…

So I was shuffled off to ACC without a clear goal and there I found some good things: I had some fine teachers. I had an interesting social life. Through the trickle-down influence of Leonard Burford I was provided a yardstick for judging excellence in the music of the Church. I gravitated into the drama department and thrived there. I saw the value of understanding and analyzing the motives of other people. This skill is essential to an actor and exceedingly useful in daily living.

And I defaulted into Lemoine Lewis's Freshman Bible Class. I use the term defaulted because I caught on during Orientation Week that the most popular Bible courses were taught by Carl Spain. I tried to sign up for his class, but it was full, so I went for what I *thought* was the second choice. Lemoine was fresh from Harvard—enamored with learning—and a gifted and inspiring teacher. For the first time I saw a coherent through line in the Biblical literature. I began to get a sense of the wholeness of the revelations that unfold within its pages. I made A grades. But I really didn't have an idea that I was noticeable to him as a student until years later when my daughter was in his freshman class and she aced a test. He told her that I was one of the best students he'd ever had.

Now this was the era in which preacher students started following Lemoine's example and going East to graduate school. In recent years at a CSC conference I heard for the first time this cohort referred to as "Lemoine's Boys." It struck me forcibly that in the 1950s, there weren't any "Lemoine's Girls." There was no one at ACC who steered me into the path of religious scholarship.

After my freshman year in college Maurine and I spent the summer in the Boston area with Paula and her husband who were already members at Brookline Church of Christ. In short order, Brookline became my favorite congregation. Through these people (some of them Lemoine's boys) I got a more accurate picture of the role of heavy-duty scholarship in the understanding and the carrying out of the implications of the gospel. I helped with children's classes and Vacation Bible School. Paula and Dennis were friends with the Malherbes. Phyllis and Abe remained our family friends through the rest of their lives.

But despite the attraction of what I was hearing, and despite a few prods from Abe, I saw no practical way for me to pursue graduate education in religion and use what I learned and stay a member of the Church of Christ.

I finished my degree in Speech and Drama at ACC with minors in English and Education and set out to be a teacher. Lanny Hunter and I married before our Senior year. After graduation we went to Kansas City for Lanny to attend Medical school. The Overland Park Church was our base in Kansas City.

The first of our four children was born just before we moved to Houston for Lanny's internship, then he was drafted into the Army and served for two years. I lived in Abilene for the year he was in Vietnam. My activities there included auditing Everett Fergusson's, Abe Malherbe's and Lemoine Lewis's classes. So I tucked away a really valuable amount of intellectual activity during that terrible year. And I was given support and encouragement, not just from these teachers and the Bailey family, but from the other members of the University Church.

Onward, Christian Soldiers...

Here I shall digress into what my second-hand experience of war has taught me. Many 19th century Church of Christ leaders held to the notion that a Christian's allegiance and energy should be devoted solely to the kingdom of God. Therefore one should not take part in human government—not hold office, not vote—and this stance included pacifism. Even after WWI, during the '30s and early '40s, many Christians in the middle of the country were conscientious objectors. By the time of World War II I was not aware that there was any problem with a Christian going to war. It was also at the back of my mind that being a conscientious objector was also a defensible position. This was not because I heard church-led discussions of it. It was my own understanding that we were to be Christ-like, forgive enemies, do good rather than harm to people. Therefore, it did not seem at all unpatriotic or wrong to me for someone to shoulder his convictions rather than to shoulder a gun. But I married a man who sought active military service. As a physician, he was drafted, but chose to volunteer for Special Forces and, in the 1964 buildup, he was sent to Vietnam. I came to see no justification for that war. I objected to Lanny's participation to the extent that I was capable. Then I supported him in the traditional way by keeping the home fires burning.

A Mighty Fortress Is Our God, A Bulwark...For Still Our Ancient Foe Doth Seek To Work Us Woe...

Because of my own experience and that of my children, because of getting to know the stories of some Special Forces battle veterans, I have become more and more convinced that "our Ancient Foe" is present and having good fun where wars rage; and that anyone who decides to return violence for violence is entering into a realm of evil. Even if you are on the "right" side in a "just" war, you are face to face with evil and you do not come away unscathed. Of those men I know personally, all have paid the price of permanent damage. Physical damage for some, and emotional and spiritual for some. They may identify their own sacrifice as being justified for a greater cause. That was the understanding I imbibed in my childhood during World War II. But that equation does not take into account the trauma heaped upon those who care about the warrior. Families don't participate in the glory of accomplishment, nor in the camaraderie. They often live as monuments to collateral damage. I don't comprehend how anyone can touch the destructiveness of war and pronounce it good.

In 2003, at my country's entry into the Gulf War, I joined with some others at Pepperdine in trying to understand and to protest the decision by Washington which promised an outcome frightfully similar to the Vietnam tragedy.

In Heavenly Love Abiding, No Change My Heart Shall Fear…

After discharge from the Army and two years in Kansas, Lanny started a dermatology residency in Minnesota. I continued my improvisations in education—I took the opportunity to earn an MA in Communication with an emphasis in Oral Interpretation. At the end of our three years in Minnesota, we moved to Flagstaff, Arizona. Our oldest child was then in 3rd grade. We had also accumulated a Texan, another Kansan and a Minnesotan, and our four children consider Flagstaff to be their home town.

It was a medium-sized town with a university and two small Churches of Christ when we arrived in 1971. We started with the mainstream church but it became apparent that we didn't swim well with the mainstream. Meanwhile our letter carrier, Lee Eyer, who turned out to be the tentmaker preacher of the other, the "anti-institutional" church, identified us. We got to know him and his remarkable wife, Elsie. So after maybe a year and a half we became a part of that congregation. The experience with another branch of the Church of Christ forced me to consider what a "New Testament Church" really is.

If I have ever qualified as a leader in the church, it was during those years. Jay and Pat Treat were with us for several years with his functioning as College Minister and then Preaching Minister. We did innovate: our public, Sunday morning services evolved to welcome participation by women and children, and we made some ecumenical alliances. Because of my being in a position of greater responsibility as a Deacon and Teacher and Reader and Occasional Preacher, I learned to understand how very difficult it is to be a leader in an organization in which the decisions are undertaken by the members, not embodied in a set of rules and codes. In the 2000s, that congregation dwindled away. But I know that during our years there, faith was strengthened and tolerance generated.

I finished my MA in Communication at Minnesota when I was 34. In Flagstaff, at Northern Arizona University, I earned a second MA in English Literature and, eventually, at the age of 56, a PhD in History and Political Science. These degrees have left me, not really a polymath but frightfully versatile in trivia games.

At an academic meeting in Tucson toward the end of my doctoral work I met David Baird, who later became the Dean of Pepperdine University's Seaver College. He hired me as replacement for a faculty member on maternity leave. Lanny and I liked being there, so I kept scrounging for jobs and, eventually, ended up with a full time teaching contract. After I retired from teaching, I worked as a researcher for David as wrote Quest for Distinction, his monumental history of Pepperdine University.

The involvement with former friends and new ones in the University Church in Malibu was a real affirmation for me. That church had begun a slow journey toward including women in progressive ways. So there, as In Flagstaff, I brought to the group what I have come to regard as my most valuable contribution. It combines performance ability, scholarship and spiritual respect. I believe those gifts come together in the oral reading of scripture. I taught classes in techniques. I arranged scriptures and coached readers for the worship services. And I certainly profited from church classes that were taught by fine teacher/scholars: Ron Highfield, D'Esta and Stuart Love, Danny Mathews, John Wilson, Tom Olbricht, Darryl Tippens, Jan and Richard Hughes, and others.

Another work that is meaningful to me is the opportunity I've had as a member of the board of directors of the Christian Scholarship Foundation. I've noted that the faculties of Christian colleges and universities are star-studded with scholars who have been the recipients of financial help from the Foundation. I confess that helping the cause of scholarship in this way is a vicarious fulfillment of my own desire to dig into Biblical treasures.

My Hope Is Built On Nothing Less…

At my great age, I no longer want to go to a church week after week in which my gifts are not used and not wanted.

So, why do I persist in wanting to be a member of the Church of Christ? Probably my mental DNA still holds a residue of exceptionalism, if not exclusivism. The Church is important to my perception of continuity in my life and I feel loyalty to it. I have investments there with family, friends, history. During hard times, help has come to me through the church associations and I am grateful. And through the Church of Christ I have apprehended an encompassing myth to make sense of the chaos of life. The Church has been a Schoolmaster to lead me to Christ. I am indebted to the Schoolmaster, but I no longer feel that I have to hold as final word everything that Schoolmaster told me. I may gain other insights from other tutors, from my own study and reasoning, and my emotional experiences.

O Sacred Head…O, Make Me Thine Forever, and Should I Fainting Be, Lord, Let Me Never, Never, Outlive My Love to Thee…

From my observations above, you know that I do have wishes and hopes for the direction of the Churches of Christ.

Be Thou My Vision…

I hope that the church will evolve to accept women in the full use of their gifts, taking as practice the full implications of "…neither Jew nor Greek, bond nor free, male nor female…" I hope that attention will be paid to the value of training ourselves to provide understanding and insights through reading scripture to each other. I have a strong desire that the churches of our movement seriously consider questions of war and peace. I wish that we could speak with a strong voice against the glorification of violence.

And, finally, addressing the question of unity of Christians:

The Church's One Foundation Is Jesus Christ Her Lord…

Christian unity is our founding ideal, but fragmentation has been a hallmark of our community of believers. In recent years I have witnessed the rich diversity of our movement. There are congregations with "Church of Christ" engraved on their door lintels that are very like the conscientious church of my youth. They have male leaders and adhere to practices they can defend by harking back to specific scriptural references. May the Lord bless and guard these enclaves.

Others, with "Church of Christ" on their signboards, make concessions to use contemporary music and promote pop Christian hits. They at times take the step over into the instrumental abyss. Generally, they are motivated by a desire to attract or to keep the young. May the Lord guide and bless their efforts.

There are "churches of Christ" with only a tenuous attachment to what the name implied in the mid-20th century. They fully embrace the integration of women into the official power structures. They accept fellowship with all who profess Christianity. They may promote agendas of social change through political activism. May the Lord direct them and bless them.

And, taking into account this broad spectrum of church practice, and folding into the list the other groups of the Stone-Campbell movement, may we all prosper and draw in those who need the God we serve and preach. May we accept and care for each other and for the strangers who come our way.

And shall we hope that we can all sing together in 4-part harmony?

Sing on, ye joyful pilgrims…

The Least of His Servants
by Dwain Evans

Early on Sunday mornings, Barbara and I listen to "With Heart and Voice," an hour of spiritual songs on public radio. Recently one selection was the old Negro spiritual, "Steal Away to Jesus." In the refrain, "The trumpet calls, within my soul; I ain't got long to stay here," and those words echo in my ears. I am 85. I know my time on earth is limited. "The years of our life are threescore and ten, or even by reason of strength fourscore…" the Psalmist said. I have used my allotment and then some.

By 1942, with World War 2 underway, my father found work with North American Aviation in Grand Prairie, Texas, and we moved, finally, to the Oak Cliff section of Dallas. During my high school years, I drove a delivery truck for a grocery, filling and delivering orders. We worshiped with the Hampton Place Church of Christ, where Logan Buchanan was the minister. By 1950, my senior year in high school, I had a scholarship to North Texas State Teacher's College. I came home one evening, finding no one at home, and I sat down on the front porch, reminiscing about my life. The Spirit of God intervened, and I shed tears about the kind of life I had been leading. I asked God the Father for forgiveness and resolved then and there that, God being my helper, I would go to Abilene Christian College.

After graduation, I quit my job at the grocery store and moved to Abilene to look for another job. I found work at 75 cents an hour with a roofing company; that lasted until my first semester in ACC.

At ACC, everything was different. No one had much money, and all my friends were committed Christians. I got a job with Olan Hicks at the Christian Chronicle. In January of my freshman year, I was introduced to Barbara Bass, who was then engaged to be married. When I heard that the engagement was broken, I called, and our courtship began. She liked the idea that I was a pre-med major, and we talked about going to New England where the church was weak, and I could make medicine my mission.

Yet in my junior year, I decided that I could be of greater service as a minister of the gospel, despite my limited gifts. Rudy Wyatt invited me to speak in his place at the little church in Truby, Texas. In my first sermon, I quoted every scripture I knew and some I did not, sitting down in five minutes. It was not a promising beginning.

By this time, Barbara had consented to marry me, but she had grown up vowing never to marry a preacher, and my decision to major in Bible caused such a crisis that we broke our engagement. By this time, we were too deeply in love to remain separated. I asked her to reconsider, and she did. We were married at the beginning of our senior year in ACC.

Of all the Bible majors in ACC, I was clearly the least promising, yet Overton Faubus, a professor of accounting in ACC, arranged a tryout at the Church of Christ in Coolidge, a town of perhaps 250 blacks and 500 whites in central Texas. The elders hired me at sixty-five dollars a week, saying they had enough support to last until January. Two weeks before we moved to Coolidge in 1954, the U. S. Supreme Court desegregated public schools. Our churches were not desegregated, and I felt that I must speak to that. The only text I could think of was the rich man and poor man of James 2. The rich man became the white man, and the poor man became the black man. It caused some uproar in the church; one prominent member withdrew. When I went to see him, he was standing out in the yard. Red in the face, he shook his fist and said, "Preacher, don't you never mention nigger again." I laughed, and said, "Gus, you know good and well that if it is in the Bible, I will mention it." Gus came back to church.

Barbara and I attended the ACC lectureship in February 1955 and heard J. Harold Thomas appeal for workers to come to the Northeast. Shortly thereafter, the elders of the Skillman Avenue Church in Dallas agreed to send us to a small mission point in Augusta, Maine. This work challenged us to the core. I found myself even more inadequate for the task.

I was a legalist of the legalists, but Harold Thomas, who was preaching in Bangor, Maine, constantly challenged me. Barbara gave me a copy of J. B. Phillips's translation of the New Testament epistles, *Letters to Young Churches*, published in 1957. As I read Romans 8:18, "In my opinion, whatever we may have to go through now is less than nothing compared with the magnificent future God has prepared for us," I was discovering the grace of God. This, I thought, is too good to be true. I went back to R. L. Whiteside's commentary on Romans, but it was too late for Whiteside to save me from grace.

After three years in Augusta, I said to Barbara, "There are better ways to do mission work. Let's return to Abilene, where I need to complete 6 hours of English and French for my degree and then recruit 10 families to go with us to plant a new church."

Back in Abilene, James Willeford, minister at Fifth and Highland, recommended us to the Lamar Street church in Sweetwater. We moved there in the summer of 1958. The elders at Lamar Street were not interested in mission work, but the elders at Parkway Drive in Lubbock came calling in 1959, and they were interested. We moved there to begin formulating our plans for a new church; soon, twelve families were committed. About this time, Walter Burch, who was working with the development office of ACC, came through Lubbock and visited me. He said, "Why don't you raise your goal to 30 families?" We determined that the Northeast was the neediest region. Four of us visited seven metropolitan areas and after prayer and fasting determined that the Lord wanted us to go to Bay Shore, Long Island, New York. With Walter's help and guidance, we prepared large charts proclaiming "Exodus/Bay Shore, Advancing a Bold Idea in Evangelism." I recruited a promising recent graduate of ACC, Rodney Spaulding, to travel with me. Walter introduced us to the elders of North Richland Hills church in Fort Worth, which became our sponsoring church. The charts were so large, we had to haul them in a trailer. Rodney and I traveled from coast to coast, telling the story.

Rodney and I had our support, but those who came with us had the true faith of Abraham, who "went out not knowing where he was to go." They sold their homes, quit their jobs, and moved to an area most of them had never seen. Time Magazine ran an article in their Religion Section on February 15, 1963, "The Campbellites Are Coming" with a picture of my family and some who were going with us. Richard Salmon and his wife, Carolyn, agreed to join us as our minister of education.

In January 1963, we set up an employment conference at the Baker Hotel in Dallas under the leadership of my brother, Ralph Evans, and his wife, Sue. We had major corporations from Long Island represented. We interviewed 150 people. Again, and again, we saw the Lord open doors we could never have opened. We were invited to use the Jewish Center in Bay Shore for our first meetings. Eighty-six families made the first move.

While our new building in West Islip was under construction, designed by Ralph Spencer of Lubbock, and constructed by James Hance, from one of our committed families, we rented three storefront buildings in Bay Shore. With those printed tin ceilings that reverberated sound, and with former members of Harding, Lipscomb, and ACC choruses, our singing made us think we had died and gone to heaven.

A busload of young people from North Richland Hills arrived and with Rodney's training went from door to door introducing the new church and arranging home Bible classes. More than 100 were arranged, and with Rodney's training we soon had 70 home Bible classes in session each week and all of this from storefronts. We baptized 150 in the first 18 months. In a little more than a year, we moved into our new building.

From the beginning, we determined to be a missionary church. The Park Street Congregational Church on the Boston Common in Boston, Massachusetts, was supporting more than 100 missionaries around the world. That stood out to us. They supported their program by an annual missions conference. Four of us attended their missions conference. We were blown away by the sacrifice and commitment of these missionaries. We came back to West Islip vowing to follow their example. Carl Phagan agreed to become our missions minister. Under Carl's leadership, we developed a Faith Corps program that would recruit college students to spend two years as apprentice missionaries around the world. Trained by Wendell Broom and George Gurganus in the summer, first at Harding then at ACC, these apprentice missionaries went out to Nigeria, Canada, Brazil, Jamaica, and Guatemala. Then Dr. Eugene Peterson, secretary of the World Council of Churches, called me for an interview in New York City. Out of this came an invitation to speak to the World Council of Churches in 1966. I shared the podium with Robert Raines.

Again, and again, we saw the power of the Holy Spirit at work doing what we could not do. Then came my invitation to speak to the ACC lectureship in 1966 about "Exodus with the Bible." I saw an opportunity to say something about the power of the Holy Spirit that we had witnessed. In that time and place, "mainline" Churches of Christ believed in the Holy Spirit as a retired author of the New Testament canon. As I prepared the lecture, Don Haymes worked with me in crafting it. Don had helped me to answer questions I couldn't ask, and to ask questions I couldn't answer. We still speak of such things.

In those days, we submitted our manuscript three months in advance and spoke two nights in a row, first in what is now the University Church and then in Sewell Auditorium. The manuscript was accepted; I was pleased.

I thought the first lecture had been well received. I did not know that a group of prominent preachers had visited Don Morris, the president, telling him that if that lecture were delivered again the next night, they would withdraw support from the school. I was called the next day to the office of the president, and there sat the president, the chair of the Bible department, and the bursar. The chair said, "We don't want you to give the lecture you gave last night. Just get up and tell about the Exodus." "Clearly," I responded, "I have said something contrary to Scripture; if you will correct me, I will make it right tonight." "No," they replied. "We agree with what you said, but the church is not ready for it." "Gentlemen," I said, "the church has had twenty centuries to be ready, and they are ready." The President leaned over his desk and said, "Dwain, it would be a shame for you to throw away your future in the church over a little thing like this." "This is not a little thing to me," I said. "If you don't want me to say what I said last night, you will have to get someone else to speak." After two hours, the chair threw up his hands and said, "No point in arguing further. It will do less damage to let him speak than to cancel it at this hour." With that blessing, I spoke.

Within a few days, I had a call from the chair of the Bible Department at Lipscomb. He said, "You are scheduled to speak here. That has been canceled." Then Oklahoma Christian called to tell me that my lecture at OCC was canceled and that "we don't want you on the campus." Dr. Frank Pack at Pepperdine, who had taught me at ACC, called to ask, "What on earth is going on with you?" I told him, and he said, "We want you to come to Pepperdine."

The fallout fell on the church in West Islip. We lost members over it. After this, Don Haymes, Walter Burch, and I planted the seeds for a new journal that would speak to real concerns, such as race, the Holy Spirit, the ministry of women, and mission. At last, we had a monthly periodical, Mission Journal, that would speak out about realities confronting the church.

Then one day in 1970, I walked into the house to hear my dear wife, Barbara—whom I loved more than life itself—say, "I am not going to teach school next year. You are going to decide whether you wish to support this family." By this time, I had a degree in pastoral counseling from Iona College; not only was I the preacher, I was also the marriage counselor. I heard Jesus saying, "Physician, heal yourself." I asked her, "Would you go with me to see Dr. Thomas Fogarty?" a great family therapist. She said, "I will." I thought to myself, "Hallelujah! Fogarty will get this lady straightened out in a hurry." Guess who he started on. He asked me, "What makes you think that God can't get his work done in this world without you?"

I heard him. I started looking for a job. I knew that I did not want to be a single preacher, but all my education was for ministry. Then I was offered a job with Glendale Associates, a firm on Long Island owned by Glen Paden and Dale Harper, who had become real estate syndicators. Soon I was commuting to Houston. In 1970, Houston was exploding, and we started buying property. I found a package of 20 prime properties for $24,000,000—prime properties on the west side of Houston. We purchased them. My employer said, "You have to move to Houston." At home, I asked Barbara if she was willing to move to Houston. She said, "Yes."

I was still preaching in West Islip, and there were few other places I could preach, but the Burke Road church in Pasadena was one of them. Wes Reagan and I traded pulpits. He went to West Islip for three months, and I preached at Burke Road for three months. Meanwhile, Barbara and our two daughters, Lisa and Stephanie, had found community with Bering Drive in Houston, and that is where we are even now.

In 1974, my company called all managers to New York and we were informed that they had taken chapter seven bankruptcy. That was bad news for me. I was on $575,000 of company debt. As soon as I got back to Houston, I went to see the banker. I walked out of his office, owing only $175,000.

My prayer was, "Lord, what am I going to do?" Houston was in one of its occasional recessions; I could not sell land for love or money, and that was what I knew how to do. I met with the regional director of Farmers Home Administration, a federal agency that developed housing in rural areas. A builder in Bacliff, Texas, had 30 lots to sell, and Farmers Home would finance them. Barbara and I sold our house, and with the equity, we bought those lots. So, we had lots but no money to build the model house. I put together my financial statement and went to bank after bank for financing; bankers laughed at me.

Then I walked into the office of W. G. (Sonny) Hall, owner of Security Savings in Dickinson, Texas. He didn't look at my financial statement. He simply said, "Evans, I am going to finance you." I knew once more that the Spirit of God is alive and well and working in our lives! I had my financing, but I didn't know how to drive a nail. Then, I heard about a company in Terrell, Texas, that built the house in their warehouse, brought it to you on a flatbed trailer, and with a small crane set it on your foundation. We were closed on the first day. Barbara decorated it, and we took 30 orders off that model. Suddenly, we were in the building business!

I formed a partnership with a company in the United Kingdom, Kebbell Holdings, which has continued to this day. We have developed subdivisions and built more than 300 houses—not because I was clever but because God was gracious. Barbara and I often reflect on how God has continued to open doors we could not open.

We are blessed with two precious daughters and their husbands, five grandchildren and six great-grandchildren, and for forty-seven years a precious spiritual family at Bering Drive Church of Christ. Barbara and I celebrated our 64th wedding anniversary on September 5th, and we are more deeply in love than we have ever been. Our constant prayer is *maranatha*, "our Lord come!"

Vision

I am asked to offer my vision of where Churches of Christ will be and what they will do in the next few decades. I don't know, and I don't know anyone who does. We are not given to know the future, but if we open our eyes and ears, we can know something of the past and the present. I live in hope, not in human behavior but in the LORD. I hope to see women involved in every aspect of the church's ministry and mission. Few Churches of Christ have employed women as preaching ministers, but I know that churches in West Islip, New York, and Brookline, Massachusetts, have done that. The Bering Drive church in Houston where Barbara and I worship has frequently welcomed women to preach, and women participate in every aspect of the church's work and ministry. Others are doing the same. ACU has invited Katie Hayes to preach in chapel, and speakers in the ACU "Summit" are frequently female.

I asked Don Haymes about a vision for disciples of Jesus in the twenty-first century and, among other things, he said, "Let us no longer be a white ghetto and a black ghetto of racial isolation. Let us come together as 'one body in Christ' to seek God's kingdom, to do God's will, and to become holy as God is holy. Let us do that, and the distinctions of the flesh that have so long divided us will disappear." That, in his mind, applies to divisions between men and women as well as to divisions of race, nationality, and culture. I share that vision.

Looking among the churches, I see a strong emphasis on the "apostles" of the Acts and the "epistles" toward the end of the New Testament, but little interest in the teaching of Jesus in the Gospels. As the church's focus has shifted from Jesus to itself, I can see little difference between Churches of Christ or Southern Baptists and other "denominations." I see many disciples and congregations turning toward a generic "evangelicalism" with its creeds and councils, and to the politics of a party.

I hope and pray that in this century, we will focus on Jesus, attend to his teaching, seek his kingdom, and do his will. When we do that, the church will truly be the Body of Christ. May God help us to be, as Jesus taught us, the salt of the earth and the light of the world.

Correcting Mistakes and Keeping the Faith in a Dominant Left-Wing PC Culture That Is Virulently Anti-Christian and Anti-Rational by J.J.M. Roberts

Memoirs

I was born in May of 1939, a few months before Germany's invasion of Poland and the final outbreak of World War II in Europe. I was the second of four children, a brother, A. Wayne, two years older, and two younger sisters, Nancy Strickland and Susan Blake Green. Like my brother, I was born at home on a 1,000-acre stock farm, six miles southwest of the small town of Winters, Texas. The population of Winters hovered around 2800 inhabitants, plus or minus a few hundred, for many years. It was located 40 miles south of Abilene, Texas, the closest large city (ca. 100,000), and the home of Abilene Christian College. San Angelo, about 60 miles south of Winters, was about the same size as Abilene, and both cities were shopping magnets for the rural population looking for goods and bargains that could not be found in their small towns. Most of my mother's family were members of the Church of Christ, so we attended the Winters Church of Christ. When I was a young child, we still met in an old frame building with a separate, large, open-sided roofed tabernacle outside for summer meetings. My dad and his family were Methodists, but he often attended church with my mother, and eventually became a member of the Church of Christ when I was still very young.

One of my mother's sisters, Ethel Davis, lived in San Angelo, so we often went there for a combination of shopping and visiting family. There, in a department store as a young child, I first became aware of the pervasive white racism of the time. Being thirsty, I went to the first water fountain I saw, but it was not the "white's only" fountain, and my mother gave me a good scolding. There was nothing quite like that in Winters. There was white racism, but the black population was quite small, and I had little contact with them. There was a separate and hardly equal school for the black students, and they had to sit in the balcony in the movie theater. For a time there was a large shabby, shanty town for poor blacks, but eventually, it was torn down. I do not remember any blacks in our church, and had little contact with any that I remember as a child. During my early years, Winters was full of people on the weekends, and that included a large number of seasonal migrant workers from Mexico during the spring sheep shearing and early autumn cotton picking seasons. There was also a small but significant permanent Latino population, primarily Roman Catholic. They went to school with us, played on our sports teams, and did not seem to provoke the same racial hostility sometimes directed against the blacks. Only when someone contemplated an inter-cultural marriage between White and Latino did the racism become readily apparent, and such marriages seemed equally opposed by both the White and Latino communities. Our public school was not integrated until I was in high school; when it was, it only involved three or so black students, and apart from a very small handful of white students, it was no big deal. In general, the students did not share the depth of racial prejudice that their parents exhibited.

I was baptized at the age of nine, and in contrast to many of my contemporaries, even as a relatively young child I was interested in and fascinated by the logic of our church's doctrine, and I began learning both Scripture and our tradition of interpretation by heart. This led to the experience of many anomalies. Some were immediately obvious as logical nonsense, but the full significance of many of them did not become clear to me until years later. Our family played games of all sorts, including card games, but the church frowned on cards because they were associated with gambling. Dominos, however, were okay, though there was a domino parlor downtown where people gambled every Saturday. Movies were also bad, that is until television came, and then no one preached against movies anymore. As a newly baptized member, I was eager to learn Scripture, but in our small church, there were relatively few really good teachers. There was one woman, however, Floy Hodge, who had the reputation of being the best, most informed teacher in the church, though she only taught women's classes. Wanting to learn, I asked permission to attend her class. The elders prohibited this, however, since they thought Paul was opposed to a woman, no matter how learned, teaching a baptized male, no matter how young. Even as a young kid, I thought this was utterly stupid. If women were to keep silent in church, how could they sing? If a woman was married to an unbeliever, how could she ask her theological question at home to an unbelieving spouse? The logic of this traditional interpretation was just goofy. Our church used grape juice for communion and communion trays with individual cups, but there was a small church in Norton, about 11 miles from our home, where we sometimes went to visit my parents' friends, that passed a single cup with real wine. My dad liked wine, so that did not bother him, but there was always a question of where to sit so that one received the cup as soon as possible, before the whole congregation had contaminated it with their germs. It was only years later that I learned that grape juice for communion was a liberal innovation associated with the temperance movement, and only possible late in the 19th century after the Methodist Welch had perfected the process to keep grape juice from fermenting. Moreover, the expression "fruit of the vine" was a Hebrew expression that meant "wine," since Passover, with which the expression is connected, occurs in the early spring before the grape harvest when no unfermented grape juice would have been available in antiquity. All the pseudo-learned attempts to remove real wine from Scripture were just extremely bad scholarship and special pleading based on a social agenda, not real exegesis.

Apart from the racism of the period, both of my parents were bright, hard-working, socially involved people. My father, W. Wayne Roberts, was a long-time scout leader, politically involved, and served for a time on the school board. My mother, Virgil L. (Wright), was the valedictorian of her high school class at the age of 16 and very well read. When the long, seven-year drought that ended in 1957 hit West Texas, both of them had to find outside employment to keep the farm. Despite having four children, my mother worked, first as a reporter, and then as a bookkeeper for different companies. My father drove a fuel truck as well as doing the farm work. Both of them, in their own ways, tried to shape my Christian faith. Dad was gruffer, but very direct, and I had no difficulty understanding him. Mother was gentler, but far more indirect. She used to take me on long walks together, where she would warn me of various pitfalls in life. Unfortunately, the warnings were largely ineffective, since most of the time I had no idea what she was talking about until years later. Her great love for the practical nature of the book of Proverbs, however, did make a lasting positive impression on my life.

Sometime in the early 50s or late 40s, our elders began to hire students from Abilene Christian College to serve as youth ministers, but these youth ministers were not pursuing degrees in youth ministry. A good number of them were Greek majors and very serious students of Scripture. Among them, James Wilburn, David Mickey, and particularly Lynn Huff had a direct influence on my life. The tradition continued for a number of years after I left for college, and a host of these youth ministers went on to do graduate work at prestigious schools like Harvard, Yale, Notre Dame, Emory, and the like, and some of them ended up with academic positions in such schools. Those that taught me fed my love for Scripture, and influenced my decision to attend ACC.

Somewhat by accident I became a Greek major, and my two closest friends in college, both Greek majors, were Ervin Bishop, later a missionary to Greece, and Paul Watson, who went to Yale a year after I left for Harvard. While these two were my best friends and continue to be friends to this day, it should be noted that we argued constantly and seldom agreed on any controversial issue. As a Greek major, I was strongly influenced at ACC by J. W. Roberts, Paul Southern, and Neil Lightfoot. My freshman year at ACC I was on a football scholarship and lived in the athletic dorm, but I proved too light and slow for college football, and the following summer I married my high school sweetheart, Genie L. Compton, and continued my college education on our own dime. Already in high school, I had begun to preach occasionally in little country churches, and I continued this as well as working part-time in the registrar's office and in the local post office in order to supplement my wife's bookkeeping salary. The experience in little churches opened my eyes to how churches actually worked, over against doctrinal theory. Women were not the powerless submissive figures that official dogma asserted, and reality was far messier and more complicated than church people often pretended.

In 1961, partly due to the vision of what Prof. Lemoine Lewis thought a minister needed to know and partly due to the offer of help from my rich aunt, Mrs. D. J. (Wright) Kirkham, who had heard of Harvard but not Claremont, I went off to Harvard for my graduate education. Shortly after arriving in Cambridge, Genie and I met Abe and Phyllis Malherbe and Tom and Dorothy Olbricht. I became Tom's assistant at the Natick church his last year there, and I learned to drink coffee just so I could spend more time listening to and learning from Abe. There was a large group of Church of Christ theological students at Harvard and Boston University at the time, and Abe had organized us into a monthly dinner and discussion group with financing from a wealthy patron, which for a time gave us a real sense both of freedom and mission to follow scripture in reforming the church.

At the time it was still considered dangerous for our people to go to "liberal" schools. In Texas, I was warned repeatedly of the danger. One country elder admonished me, "Try not to learn anything at Harvard." I was a little worried about the false teaching I might encounter there, but these concerns only lasted a week after the start of school. G. E. Wright, one of the most prominent biblical theologians of the time, the author of such seminal books as *The OT Against Its Environment* and *The God Who Acts,* was teaching OT Introduction. His first lecture in the course was so impressive I expected him to conclude it with an invitation song! He gave me an intellectual framework in which to understand the Pentateuch, the historical books, and the prophets, something that I had lacked before. It was an "Aha!" moment for me. Things began to fall into place that never quite fit before.

Wright was not nearly as good with the Psalms and the Wisdom books, however. His emphasis was to show the greatest possible contrast between the OT and its pagan environment, but the Psalms and Wisdom books had very close parallels in the surrounding cultures. Wright was tempted and did effectively chop these books from his theological canon. My mother's influence, however, and my belief in the entire canon, gave me an independence from my new teachers on this point. Wright's favorite books were important for formulating a collective theology, but individuals also need direction and a way to approach God, and the Psalms and Wisdom literature addressed these concerns of the individual.

I actually did my doctorate at Harvard under Thorkild Jacobsen in Assyriology with what amounted to a second major in OT. I decided to go this way partly because Jacobsen was such a great teacher, but mainly because I wanted a parallel field from the same general area and time to make sure that what I said about the OT was not just a case of special pleading out of ignorance of the surrounding cultures.

When my wife, three young daughters, M. Kay Thurston, Amy B. Barzdukas, and Susan R. Tipton, and I left Cambridge for my first teaching position at Dartmouth, where I finished my dissertation, and then at Johns Hopkins, where I taught for 9 years, I began to experience a rapidly changing world that was becoming more complex and messy. This was the contentious period of the Vietnam War, radical student protests, often with a gullible Marxist orientation, widespread drug use, and free love. The sexual revolution of the 60s brought with it a radical change in behavior, and the radical change in sexual behavior eventually produced a change in biblical interpretation to justify the new patterns of sexual behavior prevalent even among clergy and divinity school students. Scripture had not changed, and the historical Paul had not altered his views, but there was enormous pressure to erase the obvious conflict between the demands of Scripture and the actual sexual behavior of those who claimed to value Scripture. One need only look at historical works on Jewish or biblical sexual ethics written before the sexual revolution, and those written after it. Prior to the sexual revolution, there is little if any difference between the historical treatment of this topic between liberal and conservative scholars, whether Jewish or Christian. After the sexual revolution, the gap becomes especially pronounced, and almost none of it is based on genuinely new evidence despite claims to the contrary. One simply wanted theological approval for once proscribed sexual behavior, because too many "religious" people were going to indulge in this behavior regardless of what a genuinely historical reading of the biblical text might say.

Both my personal life and my teaching career had its ups and downs. I did a poor job in negotiating a salary for the position at Johns Hopkins, and I was always underpaid there, so we struggled to make ends meet. Nathaniel James, my only son, born in Baltimore, was killed in an automobile accident at the age of six, and the same year, despite strong departmental support, I was denied tenure at Hopkins. The next year we emigrated to Canada for what we thought was going to be the rest of our lives so that I could teach at the University of Toronto, but within a year I was called to Princeton Theological Seminary as a tenured, full Professor of OT. The twenty-five years at PTS were glorious, heady years of respect and prosperity, but even there life had its rough edges. Genie, my wife of 35 years, died of an incurable disease after a ten-year-long and very private but painful illness. In 1994 I remarried and eventually took an early retirement to be with Kathryn L. (Bloemers), my second wife, now of 24 years, who was teaching in Austin at the time.

While in Austin, I was able to restudy the thorny issue of the role of women's ministry in the church to address the issues that had long nagged at my consciousness. I taught a very well attended church-wide class at the large University Avenue Church of Christ for a period of 6 to 8 weeks. We looked at Old Testament prophecies of the Spirit being poured out equally on men and women, at New Testament references to women prophets, such as the daughters of Phillip, and to Paul's many references in his letters to prominent women in the ministry of the early church. The class was well received, but there was enormous resistance as well. The resistance was far more emotional than rational, and many of the dominant spokespersons for the resistance were women, not men. Even many of those who were intellectually convinced by my argument had emotional reservations about making any changes in our practice. The elders did agree to expand the role of women in public worship, though the changes were far more modest than I would have preferred. Even those modest changes, however, were enough to cause a significant group to switch membership to other congregations.

After the final class in the series, one of a group of women who supported my argument posed a question to me that has bothered me ever since: "Now that we have given full acceptance to women, when are we going to give the same rights to homosexuals?" This Spring, I was privileged to lecture at Calvin College in Grand Rapids and had an opportunity to take up the same issue. I noted that Paul in Galatians 3:27-28 said, "As many of you as were baptized into Christ have clothed yourselves with Christ. There is no longer Jew or Greek, there is no longer slave or free, there is no longer male and female; for all of you are one in Christ Jesus." Paul did not add, as do some ministers I have heard, "there is neither straight or gay; for all of you are one in Christ Jesus." Given Paul's clear condemnation of all forms of active homosexuality in Romans 1:18-32 and in 1 Corinthians 6:9-10, it is clear that the historical Paul did not approve of homosexuality or regard it as equivalent to being male or female. Nonetheless, I was challenged by a person in the audience, who insisted that the church should ordain and accept ministers who are involved in monogamous same-sex relationships. Neither of us relented, but it was only afterwards that I realized that the presupposition behind the question was false. The questioner really did not care whether such a minister maintained a monogamous bond. The underlying assumption, to put it crudely, was simply: "If one has a sexual itch, one must be allowed to scratch it." Neither Jesus nor Paul seems to have shared that assumption. When Jesus forbade the easy divorce of his day in Matt 19:3-12, his disciples suggested that then it was better not to marry, but Jesus dumped cold water on their response by implying that the alternative was a life of celibacy. The legitimacy of divorce in response to serious transgression is more murky as the variation in the Gospel traditions indicate, and Paul further amended those traditions, when he said that a Christian married to an unbeliever was no longer bound if that unbeliever wished to depart. The clear implication being that the believer was then free to remarry in the faith. But nothing in either Jesus' sayings or in Paul's imply that a person was free to satisfy a sexual need outside the bond of traditional heterosexual marriage. Nor is there any indication that either Jesus or Paul thought that a married heterosexual whose spouse was incapable of sex because of injury or illness was then free to satisfy their sexual needs with some substitute partner. Adultery or fornication remain proscribed. Contrary to a Lutheran graduate student who once told me that God doesn't care with whom we have sex, Jesus and Paul both seemed to care a great deal. If one wants to remain rooted in the authority of Scripture, one cannot play fast and loose with it.

To resume the narrative, Kathryn and I eventually retired to Grand Haven, MI, her home town, though for a few years I continued to serve brief terms as a Visiting Professor at various schools. My point is that if one lives long enough, along with one's successes, one will also experience unexpected and unexplained tragedies and failures in one's life. My long study of Scripture gave me resources to deal with those tragedies, though it did not answer, "Why?" and in my wildest imaginations I never foresaw the directions my life took, and I might add, continues to take.

Scripture is not as simple as we supposed, and it does not provide a ready answer for every question life throws at us. Many life decisions have to be made, if we are honest, without any clear and unequivocal direction from God. Nor is it obvious that a different decision would have been better or worse, though one's life would certainly have been different. On the other hand, Scripture is clear enough on things we should or should not do. Any serious student of the

Bible usually knows when he or she is sinning, even if we try to justify our actions by elaborate rationalizations. Few of us qualify as the simpleton of Proverbs who does not realize where his actions are taking him. At a deep level we know, we just don't care, and thus pretend otherwise.

Vision

In my vision for the future of our church within the larger Christian communion, I would like to see us transcend the racism of the past with genuinely integrated churches. In the small (60 member) Churches of Christ I attend in western Michigan this is happening. The Beeline Church of Christ in Holland has a large, fully integrated Hispanic membership as well as at least one regular black member in a non-black neighborhood. The church in Muskegon in a dominantly black neighborhood has about an equal mix of black and white members who appear to work very well together both in leadership roles and as members.

For this to continue to develop in a positive way, however, one must reject the politically correct but obviously pernicious lie that white racism is still as widespread and destructive as ever. No honest person who lived through the genuinely racist past can really believe that nonsense without a gullible suspension of reason. If there is a pervasive racism in mainstream culture today, it is black racism, which is just as pernicious and evil as white racism. The contemporary problems in the black community are not rooted in continuing white racism, but in the collapse of the black family following the destructive welfare reforms of the great society. Blaming whites for blacks' criminal convictions that far transcend their statistical portion of the general population, or for their statistically subpar academic achievements, does not address the real problem, and the contemporary demands of some black university groups for segregated black safe-spaces show how foolish this charade has become.

I would also like to see the full acceptance of women into all the ministries of the church, a move that would bring us into closer conformity to the practices of the New Testament church, but I would like to see us do that without the gratuitous assumption that the full acceptance of women is somehow intrinsically linked to an acceptance of the LGBT agenda. There is no need to compromise the clear sexual ethics of the New Testament in order to appease the incessant bullying of the homosexual lobby.

Finally, I would like to see us maintain our commitment to first-rate biblical and historical scholarship based on the study of the primary sources in the original languages in continued sympathetic but critical dialogue with our distinctive religious tradition. My greatest fear is that we will simply abandon Scripture and any of our distinctive positions rooted in Scripture, not because a rigorous study of the sources leads us to that conclusion, but because of intellectual laziness, a desire to fit into the broader religious culture more effortlessly, or in pursuit of illusory Mega-church crowds. When I say intellectual laziness, I mean preparing for ministry on the cheap, without equipping oneself with the linguistic and exegetical skills to truly evaluate competing interpretive claims. Today's youth ministry may be killing the church. Whatever the precise motivation, such a development would result in our tradition ceasing to exist in any meaningful sense. There are already indications that such an outcome is a very real possibility.

Memoirs
by John T. Willis

My wife Evelyn and I are honored that we have been invited to write our memoirs and cast a vision of the future of the Stone-Campbell Movement.

John was born in Abilene, Texas, on 21 November 1933. My father graduated from Abilene Christian College in 1928 with a Church of Christ background. He taught math at Abilene High School and was superintendent of an Abilene school. Then he bought an Office Supply Company. My mother graduated from Trinity College with a Presbyterian background. Her father was a Presbyter in the Presbyterian Church in Mansfield, Texas. Up until I was 13, we did not attend church much, but when we did, we attended the Central Presbyterian Church in Abilene. In 1947, we went to Highland Church of Christ, where I was baptized. During high school and college, we had a farm of 160 acres near Cross Plains, where I worked with cattle and plowed and sowed and harvested wheat. I fished often, continuing after we married and we had four children.

I graduated from Abilene High School in 1951 as valedictorian and graduated in Abilene Christian College in 1955 majoring in Greek as salutatorian, and in 1956 with a Master's Degree in the Hebrew Bible. I preached for four years at the Truby Church of Christ, and for three years was on the radio each week. In 1951-1956, we built strong relationships with several fellow students. These include Everett and Nancy Ferguson (Everett excels in early Church History), Abe and Phyllis Malherbe (Abe taught 10 years at ACC and taught 40 years at Yale University, a major scholar in 1-2 Thessalonians), Jim and Nona Sue

Sheerer (Jim was my best man, he served in the military at Guam a few years, and preached several decades at Chickasha, Oklahoma, now deceased), Garth and Doris Black (Garth wrote an important book on the Holy Spirit and preached several decades at Bakersfield, California), Robert and Willora Oglesby (Robert preached at the Waterview Church of Christ in Richardson, Texas, for 52 years, now retired, and is on the board of Restoration Quarterly), and Bob and Doris Vance (Bob and Doris spent several years as missionaries in Germany, and later Bob preached in Nashville, Tennessee; Bob was an extraordinary pianist; he is now deceased).

On 27 January 1956, Evelyn and I married. We met and dated 15 months at ACC. I was not in a club, but Evelyn was in Zeta Rho and attended her major events at Zeta Rho. In August 1956, we moved to Nashville, Tennessee, to teach at David Lipscomb College and get a Ph.D. at Vanderbilt. Within five years, we had four children: three sons and one daughter. David is 61 and is a missionary in Pago Pago, American Samoa. Previously he was a teacher and principal in several schools. He has six children. Debbie is 60 and has three children. Tim is 58 and has three children. Paul is 57 and has two children. We have 14 grandchildren and 7 great-grandchildren. Several more great-grandchildren are on the horizon. In 1971, we had the opportunity to present a scholarly paper at Uppsala, Sweden; Evelyn and I traveled with our four children when they were in the sixth, seventh, eighth and ninth grades going from Reykjavik, Iceland, to Luxemburg, where we rented a VW Bus with camping gear and drove and camped from Luxemburg to France to Switzerland to Germany to Denmark to Sweden to Belgium and back to Luxemburg for a month. We enjoyed visiting zoos, museums, famous sites, and interesting activities.

After our children married and moved away from home, every other year we hosted a family reunion in Flagstaff, Arizona; Los Angeles, California; Nashville, Tennessee; Taos, New Mexico; twice at Red River, New Mexico; Galveston, Texas; Possum Kingdom Lake, Texas; we took our children and spouses on an Alaskan Cruise for one week, during which time we saw a place in Juneau where millions of salmon spawned each year, saw the Mendenhall Glacier, went on a train ride in the mountains, went through the Butchart Gardens in Victoria, British Columbia, and enjoyed food and shows on the ship.

We taught at Lipscomb from 1956 to 1971 and got a Ph.D. at Vanderbilt in Old Testament in 1966. I preached at the Maple Hill Church of Christ in Lebanon, Tennessee, from 1956-1960, and at the Pennsylvania Church of Christ in Nashville from 1960-1965.

My professors at Vanderbilt made a great impact on my life, perceptions, and purposes. Kendrick Grobel taught me Greek and New Testament studies; he was a key figure in the Society of Biblical Literature for many years, and translated the two-volume theology of Rudolf Bultmann into English. J. Philip Hyatt taught me Hebrew, Hebrew Bible literature (especially the prophetic literature), and Akkadian. Lou H. Silberman taught me Hebrew, the Dead Sea Scrolls, and the diversity of the Pharisees. Bard Thompson taught me Church History. Egon Gerdes taught me Latin and Reformation History and Theology. Sven Flygt taught me Swedish, enabling one to read Norwegian and Danish. Walter Harrelson taught me form criticism, traditio-historical criticism, redaction criticism, and Hebrew Bible literature; he wrote an introduction to the Old Testament.

Many of my fellow-students at Vanderbilt have become lifetime friends. Jim Crenshaw wrote his dissertation on the doxologies in Amos, and became a professor for many years at Vanderbilt and elsewhere majoring in Wisdom Literature: Job, Proverbs, Ecclesiastes, Ben Sira, Wisdom of Solomon. Fred Craddock wrote several books and articles in the New Testament and became famous for his outstanding preaching. One year, he spoke at ACU and preached at Highland. Gerhard Hasel, a member of the Seventh-Day Advent church, was a major force in Andrews University, and was responsible for the success of Andrews University Journal. He wrote *Old Testament Theology: Basic Issues in the Current Debate*, expanded and revised to the fourth edition. Gene Boring majored in New Testament, and has written significant books and articles on Luke-Acts, New Testament prophecy, and a New Testament theology. He taught at TCU for many years.

In 1971 we began teaching at Abilene Christian College until retiring in May, 2017. So, we have attempted to teach New and Old Testament classes for 61 years with an emphasis on Old Testament, taught Hebrew and Greek and all areas of the New and Old Testaments. ACC changed to ACU about 1977. We taught undergrads and grads for many years. We are greatly honored by many students who have moved on and excelled in their field. These include Pat Graham (now at Emory University), Steve McKenzie (now at Rhodes College), Rick Marrs (now Provost at Pepperdine University), Kent Brantley (now well-known doctor about Ebola), Ken Cukrowski (now dean of the Bible Department at ACU), our son Tim (recently Dean of the Bible Department at Pepperdine University), Kathy Pulley (longtime professor and administrator at Southwest Missouri University, Springfield, Missouri); Rodney Ashlock (now chairman of the undergraduate program at ACU), Max Lucado (missionary in Rio de Janeiro, Brazil for five years, longtime preacher at the Oaks Church of Christ in San Antonio, Texas, and world-renowned biblical writer), Jennifer (Haltom) Doan (the first woman who became President of the ACU Student Body, now a lawyer), Sue Chalk (wife of John Allen Chalk, former preacher at Highland), Shanta Pundit Murray (vice-president of the ACU Student Body and now a lawyer in Tennessee), Paul Pollard (long time teacher at Harding University in Searcy, Arkansas), Rodney Cloud (long time teacher at Lipscomb), Prentice Meador (teacher and preacher, now deceased), Jim Mankin (teacher and preacher, now deceased).

In the 1970s and 1980s, the Bible faculty bussed on Sundays six times a year going to Dallas, San Antonio, Austin, etc. to preach on Sunday inviting parents and prospective students to come to ACC (ACU) at the churches where we preached. On one occasion, five of our Bible faculty members flew to Waco to have a meeting with professors at Baylor University to secure a large number of books from Baylor for the ACU library. Four times a year, six Bible faculty members and their wives went to a regional meeting at Texas Christian University for fellowship and scholarly discussions. These included Tom Olbricht, James Thompson, J. D. Thomas, etc. We gave and responded to scholarly papers on those occasions. In those days, we had good fellowship and discussions with E. Earle Ellis, Roy Melugin, David Gunn, Ron Clements, Bill Farmer, Claudia Camp, Toni Craven,

Prescott Williams, Bill Bellinger, Stephen Reid, Bill Walker, Richard Nelson, etc.

In 1966, I became a member of the Society of Biblical Literature, and became a longtime member of the Isaiah Seminar, over the years, presenting many papers in regional and national conventions on various Old Testament topics. These include scholarly papers at Toronto, Canada, Chicago, Boston, Atlanta, Kansas City, Kansas, San Diego, New Orleans, San Antonio, San Francisco, Seattle, Washington DC, and Orlando. In the Society of Biblical Literature, we are longtime colleagues of Walter Brueggemann, Hugh Williamson, Chris Francke, Gary Stansell, Roy Ward, Jimmy Roberts, Ken Kuntz, C. L. Seow, etc. Pat Graham, Rick Marrs, and Steve McKenzie edited 15 essays in Worship and the Hebrew Bible. Essays in Honor of John T. Willis. JSOTS 284; Sheffield: Sheffield Academic Press, 1999, listing the scholarly publications up until that time. A few years ago, Evelyn and I hosted Walter Brueggemann at ACU for a series of his lectures.

I had the opportunity of presenting scholarly papers in the International Organization for the Study of the Old Testament in 1971 at Uppsala, Sweden, and in 1985 in Jerusalem, Israel. In Uppsala, we were in the home of Helmer Ringgren, collaborating to translate several articles of Ivan Engnell from Swedish into English, now published as A Rigid Scrutiny. There we first met David Clines, instigator of the Journal of Old Testament Studies, and author of a theological lexicon with many volumes, and Leslie Allen, who has written many scholarly commentaries on the Hebrew Bible, now professor of Fuller University in California. In Jerusalem, we first met Chris Begg, general editor of Old Testament Abstracts leading to be a longtime associate editor of OTA, writing numerous books and articles on Old Testament topics, many of which are listed in various books.

In 1985, we became a member of the Catholic Biblical Association of America, there presenting numerous papers, being a long time member of the Divinity Seminar, presenting scholarly papers at The Catholic University of America in Washington DC; Creighton University, Omaha, Nebraska; Notre Dame University, Notre Dame, Indiana; Loyola University of Los Angeles, California; Providence College, Providence, Rhode Island; Catholic University in Halifax, Nova Scotia; Catholic University in New Orleans, Louisiana; Gonzaga University in Spokane, Washington. Some of our longtime colleagues in this organization are Mark Smith, Dale Launderville, Corrie Corvalho, Randy Chesnutt.

Evelyn and I have traveled all over the world many times. We have been to all fifty USA states and 34 foreign countries. We taught extended classes for ACU in Sao Paolo, Brazil; Dallas, Houston, Lawton, Oklahoma; Wichita Falls, Atlanta, Georgia; Accra, Ghana; St. Petersburg, Russia; twice in Nairobi, Kenya; and held seminars twice in Singapore, twice at the annual Asian Forum in Chiang Mai, Thailand, twice in Brazil—in Vittoria and Porta Allegra; Gabarone, Botswana; Uk Pom near Calabar, Nigeria. We taught Hebrew Bible classes at the South Pacific Bible College in Tauranga, New Zealand ten times over the years, each time for a month. The people there are Maori. We attended Maori shows, and became friends with several Maori people. The two major industries in New Zealand are timber and shepherding. Several times we went to the Agrodome to learn about the wide diversity of sheep and their wool, and the work of shepherds, from which we learned much about the function of shepherds in the church. One year we went with Scott and Joy Harsh and Dan Allen to Hobbiton, the site of The Hobbit. Scott took many pictures, and put together a very nice booklet with many of the pictures which we took there. We spent a day at the Auckland Zoo, where we took pictures of Keas and Kiwis. New Zealand people call themselves Kiwis, the national bird is Kiwi, and a major fruit is Kiwi. ACU assigned us to take ACU students on archaeological excavations 1992, 1994, and 1995, where we served at Banias in North Israel just below Mount Hermon six weeks each. During those years, we baptized three students from Pepperdine University in the Jordan River.

In 1978, Evelyn and I went with Wendell Broom to Lagos, Calabar and UkPom, Nigeria. There we worked with Bob and Joan Dixon at UkPom, missionaries there for approximately 25 years. We held a three-night revival, resulting in 103 people obeying the gospel being baptized in the river. Joan's maiden name is Snell. One of her sisters is Jan Snell, who married David Brantley. One of their children is Kent Brantley. In 2002, Dan McVey and I went to Tanzania to work with a young couple to begin their missionary work there. This country is approximately 98% Muslims. During that time, we went on a boat for about two hours to go to the Island of Zanzibar, where a guide led us through the spice farms. In Kenya, we spent several nights in a large tent at Masai Mara, and spent each day standing in a landrover to see the animals in the safari, including elephants, lions, cheetahs, zebras, wildebeests, hyenas, giraffes, dik-diks, gazelles, etc. In Singapore, we went to the Singapore Zoo and had breakfast with an orangutan and her baby. We observed the crocodile show in which the trainers carried crocodiles on their backs; one trainer opened the mouth of a crocodile, went inside its mouth with his head to drop a dollar bill on its tongue and later went back into the mouth with his head to pick up the dollar bill up with his teeth. After the show, we held a crocodile on our laps sitting in two chairs side by side to get a picture holding the crocodile. Ken Sinclair, a long time missionary and friend in Singapore and Malaysia, was our host.

Evelyn and I were honored at an annual lecture at Pepperdine University in Malibu, California, and at an annual conference of the Christian Scholars Conference in Nashville, Tennessee.

In a little over six decades of teaching at Lipscomb and ACC (later ACU), thousands of students have blessed us tremendously. We were honored as Teacher of the Year at ACC in 1974 and at ACU in 2005. Even though our teaching was in the Bible, we intentionally encourage students of all fields to be faithful to God and to pursue their gifts and desires to serve all people as opportunities arise. We had numerous students in our home over forty years on Sunday night fellowship events. We entertained over 80,000 students in our home, at least 40,000 different individuals. It is a great blessing to know the marvelous successes of many of these wonderful students and their families. Through the years, many GA students and Peer Leaders have worked to deal with a wide variety of students in all fields.

When Evelyn and I were engaged, we prayed together every day except a few times when we were separated geographically. In 1961 I went with a team of about 40 people to visit from house to house in London to establish the Wembley Church of Christ. The preacher to begin that work was Philip Slate. Through the years, we have placed great emphasis on the importance of the family. In the 1980s Randy and Camilla Becton headed up an effort called "Saving the American Family." About 300 to 400 people from a wide range of churches would meet every year for about three days in Dallas to make presentations about family issues. We were always closely connected with Paul Faulkner and Carl Brecheen, who spent many years presenting family situations in seminars all over the USA and beyond. On July 30-August 3, 2011, Evelyn and I participated in the Asian Forum in Chiang Mai, Thailand, speaking three times in the forum, and Paul and Carl gave their presentations to the participants there. There were about 280 people who attended that forum. At the present time, we have a program at Highland called "Re-Engaged," encouraging couples to meet for about ten weeks to relive and reignite their marital relationship.

Evelyn and I participated in shepherding the Highland Church of Christ for 42 years (since 1976). Through those years, we have had between 30 and 40 shepherds. We have faced all kinds of good and bad issues. We have tried to protect our preachers and staff and all the members of the church whom we serve. Different shepherds serve as chairman for a year or two. John was chairman in 2000, the year when the whole church began expanding the role of women, which has led to a very healthy spiritual growth. We now have three campuses which meet every week. In 2017, 215 people were baptized into Christ. We are presently working on helping the homeless, expanding mission works, dealing with sex trafficking issues in the USA and abroad, and trying to encourage everyone to be faithful disciples of Jesus. At the present time, we are adding several new shepherds to our group. We intentionally think of couples (husband and wife) in the eldership working together, not of individuals. Our role is not to lord ourselves over the flock, but to make ourselves examples under the Chief Shepherd, Jesus Christ (1 Peter 5:3-4). When people have physical, emotional, social, and spiritual problems, we bring them into the shepherd's meetings so that we can anoint them with oil, wash their feet, pray for and with them, study the Bible with them, and support and encourage them in every way we can. God's faithfulness sustained us during good and bad situations. It is obvious that God has sustained us faithfully.

VISION

It is presumptuous for any individual or any group of people to know what the future holds and make definite plans for the future. GOD ALONE knows the future and holds the future in his hand. Ecclesiastes 5:3 says: "God is in heaven, and you upon earth; therefore let your words be few." The best Evelyn and I can do is to wish and hope that God will carry out his plans and purposes. From our very limited perspective, we would like for several things to happen.

Since God is the Living God, we must look to him for discernment and help in all our thoughts and decisions. Every day, we must pray fervently to God to glorify God in everything we attempt to think, say, or do. Since God has given us his revealed message, we must repeatedly study the Bible, meditate on God's words, and attempt to do what God guides. Ezra diligently followed this routine: "For Ezra had set his heart to study the Law of the Lord, and to do it, and to teach the statutes and ordinances in Israel" (Ezra 7:10). Jesus emphasizes this principle in the Sermon on the Mount: "Everyone then who hears these words of mine and acts on them will be like a wise man who built his house on the rock" (Matthew 7:24). If we are serious about this, we must have well-trained people to learn Hebrew, Aramaic, Greek, ancient Near Eastern archaeology, biblical theology, early Church History, etc. to keep all of God's people up to date on the issues we face daily. As we worship a God of peace, we must all strive to accept and love one another. This includes not merely Church of Christ people, but all people on earth. This is the prayer which Jesus declared in John 17:17-26. All sincere people desire to learn and follow God through Jesus Christ. As limited human beings, we will always differ on various issues. It is very important for each individual to share his/her personal views, but when everything is said and done, we must listen to the views of others and respect and love one another.

In daily personal living and church living, it is imperative that we follow Jesus' two Great Commandments: Love God with all your heart, soul, mind, and strength, and Love your neighbor as yourself (Matthew 22:34-40; Mark 12:28-34; Luke 10:25-28). Hopefully, this will help all genuine disciples—followers of Jesus—to expand our collective views of loving people of all races, backgrounds, and cultures, including everyone, men, women and children in all church activities, of supporting, encouraging, and transforming the anxious, fearful, depressed, needy, poor, disabled, homeless, addicted, forgotten, rejected, and enemies.

Committed Christian individuals and churches must be heavily involved in all levels of activities in the city, state, and nation. We need Christian lawyers, judges, coaches, doctors and nurses, presidents, deans, governors, senators, congresspersons, social workers, business people, pilots, day laborers, waiters and waitresses, teachers, preachers, librarians, tutors, mentors, youth ministers, counselors.

Memoirs of an Old Ball Player
by Gail E. Hopkins

There are a lot of ways I could organize this essay about the formative factors and influences that have led me to where I am today. Because I am a believer in Jesus and his teachings as found in the Bible, I see no acceptable way of separating my spiritual life in him from what some might call the various parts, or jobs, or aspects, or accomplishments of my life. In other words, in my view, my spiritual life in Christ is simply all of my life. I cannot separate it into compartments that somehow are devoid of Jesus' influence and presence. God has been with Caroline and me all the way! Thus, when I contemplate how I got to where I am, I hope to show you that the important factors and people in my formation are in reality pretty simple and straight forward.

Let me discuss a few parts of the life that Caroline and I have shared before I address the substantial matters of my formation. I was probably asked to participate in this discussion group because of my life as a professional baseball player for 14 years. Additionally, my work as an Orthopaedic surgeon, my involvement in Christian higher education, and my involvement as a member of the Church of Christ are areas of lives where Caroline and I have lived out our shared faith life. Involvement in these four aspects of my life has been very rewarding personally to both of us. They have certainly influenced how and where Caroline and I have lived, and the things we have done in life. However, I do not think these four parts are the major factors that have shaped my personal faith life. The first three of these aspects are certainly important parts of our shared life, but I was who I am before professional baseball, medicine, or higher education. My involvement with the church of Christ is a different matter. I hope to make this clear as I proceed through this essay.

I want to comment briefly about each of the first three factors before getting to the meat of my formation. In the immortal words of Bill Dana's Jose Jimenez or SNL character Chico Escuela, "Baseball, berry, berry good to me!" In my 14 years of playing baseball for money, one of the many things that I learned from baseball is that trick plays do not really work. In professional baseball, the experienced players all pretty much know what the most likely and best statistical play will be in a given situation. Trick plays usually work only if and when the opposing manager does something that is fundamentally unsound, such as change a bunt play to something that is not consistently reproducible. In professional baseball, players and teams do not succeed by going against the time-tested fundamentals of the game.

There are some real lessons for life in this observation, which would be fun to unpack, but not today. Successful athletes in all sports follow the fundamental rules and principals of the sport, such as in baseball of always watching and knowing where the ball is.

Similarly, as an Orthopaedist treating an open (compound) fracture, my patient does not fare well if I neglect following fundamentals of care, such as irrigating and debriding the wound, proper antibiotic application, proper fracture fixation, and stabilization, adequate medical and surgical follow up, and proper physical rehabilitation. Unless I cover all these steps and more, the patient is likely not to do well.

Just as I have observed that it is important to follow the principals and fundamentals of baseball and Orthopaedic surgery, I think that it is analogously important to apply solid fundamentals to life in general. For instance, doing stupid things in baseball leads predictably to a bad result, just as doing dumb things in life, such as not wearing your seatbelt while driving your car, leads to predictable bad injuries. Sometimes you can do everything correctly by following best principles and practices, yet unfortunately, the outcomes or results are not what one wanted or expected.

This observation is true not only of life but also of baseball and surgery. Following fundamentals, principals, and best practices does not guarantee the outcome one might want, but it does give you the best chance of success. The Bible clearly teaches that bad things happen to good people. For instance, the rain falls on both good and bad people no matter what they do or do not do. There are some things in life, often many things, which are truly out of our control. However, just as with both baseball and surgery, if you do things the best fundamentally sound way, you are likely to have a better result than doing things in unsound ways. The same observation holds for our individual and corporate relationship to the Lord and his church.

It is difficult for me to completely separate my service to God within his church from my efforts to support Christian higher education. As to my roles in Christian education, just as I discussed the importance of following fundamental principles and rules in baseball and surgery, I have striven to follow solid education and Christian fundamentals and doctrine. Because I like predictability in the things that I do, whether I have functioned as a student, faculty member, donor, board of trustees or regent member, or as chair of the university, I have looked for fundamental principles to guide me.

My first actual contact with Christian higher education occurred at the Pacific Bible Seminary in Long Beach, California. As a senior in high school, I took night classes at PBS in order to learn more about God and the Bible. When I graduated from high school, I went off to Pepperdine College in 1961 because I could study Bible and biology. I accepted a full scholarship to play basketball and baseball at Pepperdine College. Were it not for athletic and academic scholarships, I would not have been able to attend Pepperdine College or any other college or university in those years. My parents had no financial ability to pay for my higher education; however, God had plans for me, which I did not understand at that time. I had decided not to accept full scholarships to the University of California at Berkeley or Stanford University. I had decided to stay at home in Long Beach and go to Long Beach Junior College.

That was when God brought Henry Barnhart, my junior high school teacher and coach, back into my life. Barney called my mother one day in May 1961 and talked with her. On a Saturday morning, Barney came by my house and picked me up in his convertible MG. We drove the 13 miles to Pepperdine College's campus, where he had already arranged a meeting with the Athletic Director and staff. He explained to me why I was going to go to Pepperdine. One did not argue with Mr. Barnhart! Plus, everything he said made sense. It was not a hard decision to make. Before Barney took me to Pepperdine on that Saturday, I knew nothing about the school! That Saturday morning drive in Barney's MG changed everything. I will mention Barney again below.

God used Christian higher education to enrich my life profoundly. God's Spirit had been working in me from the time that I was 9 years old. God's Spirit was shaping and enriching my life in ways that I did not always understand or anticipate. The most significant thing that God did to me at Pepperdine College was that He brought Caroline Leah Shaeffer into my life when I met her on a Friday night playing recreational volleyball in the gymnasium. It turned out that she fundamentally completed me as a human being, and we have been constant companions since that Friday night. Nothing besides my baptism and being filled with God's Spirit has had more of an impact on me than Caroline.

At Pepperdine, I was also challenged intellectually and spiritually to strive for excellence as God brought different ideas and people into my life to strengthen what he had already started in me. Such Christian men and women as Gordon Teel, Michio Nagai, Norvel and Helen Young, J.P. Sanders, Carl Mitchel, Lucille Todd, Bruce M. Harrison, Warren Kilday, Lloyd Frasier, Gary Marks, Frank Pack, Howard White, Bill Kneip, and Jack Scott. Jack was part of this panel last year. He, along with so many others, instructed and helped deepen my relationship with God. In particular, Bill Green was a powerful influence on me intellectually, but especially through his humble spirit. I took about 30 credits from Bill. Because Howard White and Frank Pack awarded me a scholarship to study for my MA in Religion during the early years of my professional baseball career, I was able to meet such characters as Reinhold Niebuhr, Carl Barth, Rudolph Bultmann, Paul Tillick, Josef A Jungmann, Louis Boyer, Leonhart Goppelt and so many others. All of these Christian scholars added to what God was doing with me.

George Pepperdine, at the inauguration of his college in Southwest Los Angeles in 1937, said a couple of things that have stuck with me ever since I started my Christian higher education studies at Pepperdine. It should be obvious that I was not present at the inauguration in 1937, but I have participated in its reenactment many times at Pepperdine University's annual Founder's Day ceremonies. One part of his very succinct, yet powerful, speech accurately entails what I might call a guiding goal for my life. Mr. Pepperdine said that the work done at Pepperdine would be of great importance if it were "guided by the hand of God," and by that he meant "...that God's Spirit working through his holy word, the Bible, shall influence and control the lives of each and every member of the faculty to such an extent that he will spread Christian influence among the students." Before I ever knew anything about Pepperdine, I was absolutely convinced that I need to know more about the teachings of the Bible in order to serve the God of the Bible more effectively. That was why I went to a Christian school and not to the University of California at Berkeley or Stanford where I had full scholarships to attend if I desired to do so. Because of a series of events surrounding Henry "Barney" Barnhart, who was my teacher, coach, Pepperdine alum, and friend while growing up in Long Beach, God guided me to Pepperdine where I could study both the Bible and biology.

A second point Mr. Pepperdine made is one of the reasons that I am so committed to Christian higher education. After making the point I just mentioned, he continued by noting the following:

> *The heart of man usually grows to be perverse unless trained by the influence of God's word. If we educate a man's mind and improve his intellect with all the scientific knowledge men have discovered and do not educate the heart by bringing it under the influence of God's word, the man is dangerous. An educated man without religion is like a ship without a rudder or a powerful automobile without a steering gear.*

This comment frankly scares me when I look around the world and our country today. When I think of history and the current state of affairs in the world, I am then reminded that Jesus taught us that the world would be a mess until he comes again. It is possible to both "educate a man's mind and improve his intellect" at the same time. That was Mr. Pepperdine's goal, and it is why Caroline and I have committed to supporting Christian higher education. Our view of Christian higher education and responsible scholarship is that both are done in service to Jesus' church. Because of this idea, we support the efforts of Church of Christ universities and colleges in general and Ohio Valley University and Pepperdine University specifically. We have also supported such enterprises as the Stone-Campbell Journal, the Christian Scholarship Foundation, World Bible School, Society of Biblical Literature, the Thomas H. Olbricht Christian Scholars Conference, various Bible college lectureships, and so on.

In mentioning Thomas H. Olbricht, I must pause here to comment on Tom and Dorothy Olbricht. I was not one of Tom's students. We first met about 40 years ago. Over that time, Tom and Dorothy have become among our dearest friends, and we have traveled and interacted in each other's lives in multiple ways. I have benefitted immeasurably from Tom's friendship, and our discussions about baseball, trees, maps, food, preachers, schools, churches, theology, Restoration history, and just about any subject involved with life have been enlightening for both of us. These times and discussions have also added to my spiritual maturity. Tom and Dorothy, much like Caroline, are viewed as family and have helped polish my rough edges and helped keep me centered in my place—which is usually driving the car!

My religious roots were well planted by my parents in two of the major divisions of the American Restoration Movement. My mother grew up active in the Independent Church of Christ in Manford, Oklahoma, and my father in the Church of Christ in southern Oklahoma. It may sound presumptuous of me, but I know who formed me and who it was that influenced me to become the person that I am. When I left my parents' home at 18 years of age to go to Pepperdine, I was already fundamentally formed. I have a lot more knowledge and experience at my current age, but I am still basically the same living being that I was at 18 years old. The question of who brought me to my current place is easy to answer. It is God. There is no doubt about that fact. When I heard and believed the gospel message as taught to me by my mother's brother, Dutch, at the age of 9 years, God's Spirit entered me and transformed me and has continued to mold me to this day. Ever since that time, I have felt and always feel God's presence in my life. His Spirit has drawn me deeper into his word and in fellowship with him and his people. I cannot underestimate my sense and knowledge of God's presence through his Spirit in my life. I feel it and know he is with me just as assuredly as I feel the keys on this computer as I write these words. The most formative factor in my life has been God. It was my Uncle Dutch who introduced me to Jesus just as Andrew brought Simon to Jesus, who then completely changed both Simon's and Andrew's lives. Jesus changed me in ways that I did not always understand, but nonetheless, change me he did. He has used many people to clean and polish me. I will mention a few of the important ones now.

Even though my parents were both raised in families that regularly worshiped God, my parents did not attend worship services when I was living with them as a boy. They were good parents in providing for us in worldly ways. We were never rich, but we had the necessities of life. When I was 9 years old, it was my Uncle Dutch (Howard Reynolds) who persuaded my parents to let him take my brother Don and me to Sunday school and church at the Dominquez Church of Christ, an Independent Church of Christ. On the dash of his car was a small sign that quoted John 3:16. Dutch explained Jesus to me starting with that passage. After a few weeks, I asked to be baptized. Before being baptized, the minister Glenn Westerberg and an elder came to my house to make sure that I really understood what I was asking to do.

It may sound implausible to some, but God fundamentally changed and formed me at that time. I immediately started talking with God, asking him for help, and I have not stopped. I started carrying and reading the Bible daily. Dutch and Glenn taught me that I would find the words of God in the Scriptures. From about 12 to 15 years of age, Glenn met with four other boys and me on Sunday nights at the church building for a special Bible study. I wanted to be like Glenn and to serve God. As a high school senior, I even attended the Pacific Bible Seminary at nights to study Bible because Glenn had studied there.

However, I did not forget my Church of Christ roots. I also worshiped at times at the Uptown Church of Christ, especially during the week. The singing was amazing. This leads to another significant influence that God used in my life. I never met my grandfather, Almon Allen Hopkins, who was known as "Al." He was a preacher in the Church of Christ, mostly in Oklahoma and Texas. He preached his first sermon in 1888 and last sermon in 1937 at the Shannon Church of Christ in Sherman, Texas, where he was born. He was taken from the pulpit on a Sunday morning when he became acutely ill because of appendicitis. He died a few days later from the complications of a ruptured appendix. My father told me many stories about my grandfather. These stories profoundly impacted me and my desire to serve God. I cannot explain it, but he was a great inspiration to me and still is. I would like to say more, but space does not allow that at this time. In full disclosure, I want to let everyone know that my grandfather Al Hopkins is our session respondent Jason Fikes' great grandfather! That is pretty cool!

Finally, I want to acknowledge and thank God that he brought Caroline Leah Shaeffer into my life at Pepperdine. I cannot count the innumerable ways that God has used her to polish me. It has been a fantastic journey thanks to the manifold wisdom of God that he constantly brings to me through her. I would not be here without her.

CONCERNS FOR THE CHURCHES OF CHRIST IN THE COMING DECADES

I want to thank Gayle Crowe for inviting me to participate in these memoirs. He also asked that I cast a vision for where our fellowship of the Churches of Christ is going over the next few decades. Unfortunately, I see division being already present and growing in intensity in various locations of the country. I am not sure how it will end and to what extent it will progress. When the idea that past is prologue is applied to the Churches of Christ, our history has a lot of division and strife. However, I do not despair for the church as it is described in Scripture. Jesus has assured us that nothing will prevail against his church. Perhaps, the relevant issue is whether or not we will be part of that church described in the New Testament. The following are some of the areas or issues of concern that I anticipate will challenge the unity of and cooperation among the fellowship of the Churches of Christ over the next couple of decades.

Historically accepted exegesis, interpretations, and the application of Scripture in areas such as the acceptability of musical instrumental accompaniment in corporate worship, the role of women in public worship and pulpit preaching, and the role of women in congregational leadership as deacons and/or elders are being challenged in various sectors of the Churches of Christ. There are significant changes in the liturgy of worship, such as the informalization of worship in terms of dress, language, prayer styles, coffee, and food bars during worship, and the use of popular evangelical contemporary Christian praise and camp song types of music in place of traditional hymnals. This has led to a decreased use of four-part harmony and use of musical notes in either books or by various electronic screen projections of the songs being sung in worship. Importantly, congregations have decreased the number of times that the church comes together as a whole by eliminating Sunday evening and mid-week services in favor of small groups or eliminating these services altogether.

Quite significantly, there is an increasing lack of trained preachers because young men, in particular, are no longer going into pulpit preaching. This results from local congregations and Christian parents failing to encourage their children to consider full-time ministry. This is a problem being experienced by denominational churches also. Moreover, local churches and church families are failing to encourage their children to pursue Christian higher education. Of the approximately 18,000 high school seniors who identified with the Churches of Christ in 2018, only 2,004 attended one of the 14 Church of Christ colleges as a freshman, whereas about 4,411 of high school graduates attended one of the 14 schools in the year 2000 as a freshman (see Trace Hebert's work). Colleges are now recruiting "mission fit" co-religionists in order to pay the operational costs of the schools. This will have long term negative effects on the Churches of Christ, and its relationship to fellowship schools. Some schools will close operations while others will loosen their relationship to the fellowship. The tragedy in all this is that a generation or two of our children will be lost to the secular world, all while the remaining Church of Christ membership grays.

A final observation is that many congregations of the Churches of Christ are continuing to drift into evangelical theology and practices, and demonstrate little differences from evangelical community churches. Examples of this are the growing support for patriotism, national defense, military intervention, and support for war against the enemies of freedom. An additional example is increased congregational participation in social justice activities, such as AA and other community good social justice activities. The problem with the latter is that these justice activities are often devoid of any emphasis on sharing the gospel, which is a primary task of the church.

Most of my observations above arise because of the powerful influences on the church of secular culture, postmodern thinking, and liberation theology. In particular, liberation theology has played strongly in the rise of women in our society and culture, which has been a good thing. However, liberation theology has troubling tenants that are rarely discussed, and they pose potential negative issues for the church. Commensurate with all of this has been a depreciation of the privileged position of Christianity and its institutions in our nation.

Significantly for the Church of Christ, the position and authority of the Bible has been devalued as a standard of personal morality and cultural norms within our American society. The Bible is viewed by many as an ancient book out of step with a modern scientific society. As with the "Pirates Code" from the movie *Pirates of the Caribbean*, the Bible is viewed as "mostly, just guidelines" and not as instructions from God as to standards and rules for the Christian and non-believers in terms of morals, faith, and activities of life.

These observations presented above are offered for serious consideration and thought. I do not despair for the future. God is in control of time and his church. It should be kept in mind that the "unity" of the church is not dependent on the differences that exist among believers. Unity is a decision that believers make based on their common shared beliefs, characteristics, faith, and interests. Unity does not require uniformity. Unity may occur when not all things are uniform. Unity is based on our common faith in Jesus Christ as Lord and Savior. The

Church of Christ is a diverse fellowship; let us pray that God grants us unity and that he uses us to his glory.

Let Peace and Unity be our prayer.

About the Editors

Thomas H. Olbricht was born in Thayer, Missouri. He was educated at Harding and Northern Illinois Universities. He was awarded graduate degrees at the University of Iowa and Harvard Divinity School. He has taught at Iowa, Harding, the University of Dubuque, Penn State, Abilene Christian, and Pepperdine. He has taught as an adjunct at Lipscomb University, The Institute of Theology and Christian Ministry in St. Petersburg, Russia, Great Commission School in Nairobi, Kenya, Bible School in Marseilles, France, and South Pacific Bible College in Tauranga, New Zealand. He has written or co-edited thirty books counting a few soon to be in print. He has served as a minister in DeKalb, IL, Iowa City, IA, Monticello, AR, Natick, MA, State College, PA, and Derry, NH, and preached from over 250 pulpits throughout the world. He and Dorothy have been married 68 years. They have five children, twelve grand children and 5 great grand children. They live in Boulders, a retirement community in Exeter, NH.

Gayle M. Crowe, the son and grandson of elders in Churches of Christ, grew up in Denver, Colorado. His degrees are from Abilene Christian University, Wheaton Graduate School, Harvard Divinity School, and Harding Graduate School of Theology. His career was as a minister/pastor in Churches of Christ, with a total of thirty three years in Chatham, New Jersey, and Lafayette, Indiana. A prime interest through 40+ years has been Christian broadcasting. He left the pulpit after 42 years in 2007 and currently serves as Vice President for Programming with World Christian Broadcasting, as well as years as a shepherd with the Woodmont Hills Church in Nashville, Tennessee. He and Lisa, married since 1965, are the parents of a son and a daughter and grandparents to two granddaughters.

If you enjoyed this book, please consider leaving an online review. The authors would appreciate reading your thoughts.

About the Publisher

Sulis International Press publishes fine fiction and nonfiction in a variety of genres. For more, visit the website at
https://sulisinternational.com

Subscribe to the newsletter at
https://sulisinternational.com/subscribe/

Follow on social media
https://www.facebook.com/SulisInternational
https://twitter.com/Sulis_Intl
https://www.pinterest.com/Sulis_Intl/
https://www.instagram.com/sulis_international/

www.ingramcontent.com/pod-product-compliance
Lightning Source LLC
Chambersburg PA
CBHW052056110526
44591CB00013B/2235